The years best Scary ghost story

A Collection of 10+ Scary Ghosts Stories

The years best Scary ghost story : A Collection of 10+ Scary Ghosts Stories

BY

Kabir shikder

Contents

Chapter One

The thing that Boonie enjoyed the most about dumping off Black Bridge was how convenient it was. Take, for example, the amount of time it takes to travel. Even with small ice minefields booby-trapping Hellam's backroads, he estimated it would take him ten minutes to hump a full load of barrels from there to here in the old Dodge truck.

So even if the storm hit before they finished—with the chances of that increasing—it would only take them forty-five minutes to unload the entire batch and skedaddle back home.

He was especially grateful on evenings like these.

They hadn't seen many nights like this before.

Boonie grinned as he spat out, "Jesus." "Would you take a look at that nonsense?" He poked the clouds with one huge thumb, which hung swollen and gray in the black sky above him. His other hand held the steering wheel in a loose grasp, steering by instinct. "You know how they look like giant, dead, nasty brains? As if the entire sky is comprised of brains..."

Drew murmured from the passenger seat, his bulging lemur eyes glistening with crystal meth and worry. "Let's just go back, man," he said. "Do it the next day or something. We're not going to be able to work in this mess."

Boonie scowled as he swerved around a pothole. "Drew, you're such a fuckin' wiener. You're not fond of the storm? It's fantastic, guy."

Winter lightning twitched to God's angry snarl as the sky went kaboom and neon-flickered. Drew shivered and jumped.

It was hysterically funny. "I love this crap," Boonie said again, his eyes fixed on their target.

Black Bridge loomed large in the stormy, primordial sky in front of them. It didn't take much convincing for it to be classified as ultimate creature-feature territory. It was a rusting dinosaur from the days when trains were the lifeblood, steel rails the veins of Paradise County and the nation: a brooding, decrepit old railroad crossing, limned by crumbling stone and situated smack-dab in the middle of nowhere: a rusting dinosaur from the days when trains were the lifeblood, steel rails the veins of Paradise County and the nation.

It was overgrown, flanked by bleached bone trees, tangled with kudzu, and dense, gnarled vegetation after a generation of neglect. Many of the ties were punky and worm-holed, but the poured concrete pylons and steel beams still stood, casting fat lightning shadows on the Codorus Creek's murky green waters thirty feet below.

Toad Road, a rough, chuck-holed dirt road just wide enough to accommodate the overloaded vehicle, was the only route in. Toad Road, which snaked through a lush green valley in the county's east end, was unmarked and only featured on the county's most anal tax maps, which pretty much sealed the deal on the privacy issue. It was solely home to dopers, dirtbikers, and hunters hunting for an off-season deer or two during the day.

There was no one there at night.

Yes, Boonie adored everything about this location: the proximity, the solitude, and the eerie vibe. But it was the fact that if you parked right in the middle of the bridge and angled the sucker back till your ass hung over the side, you could just lean the barrels off the back and let go straight into the creek that he enjoyed the most. The fuckers didn't even had to get out of bed. That eliminated a lot of the really heavy lifting, which was the most unpleasant part of the task, aside from the smell.

Bradley Gene Pusser, known by his pals as "Boonie," was a twenty-five-year-old, six-foot-four-inch, two-hundred-and-seven-pound monster of ugliness. His pasty, aging-Elvis features were awful, his eyes unhappy and bulging beneath the brim of his blue Steelers cap. He'd inherited the Pusser genetic proclivity for drunkenness, pattern baldness, and fat, in addition to his size and vicious demeanor.

Since the end of his high school football career, his life had been a steep, brutal downhill slope. Back in the glory days, he'd been able to indulge his dreams of scholarships, pro ball, and a permanent all-expense-paid ticket out of this scumbag town. His coach believed, his teammates believed, the nookie-nookie candyass cheerleaders believed, and goddamn if his owndaddy—the venerable Otis J., Jr.—didn't feel a Pusser had been born who could break the chain and bust on through to some kind of success.

But, late in his senior year, his right kneecap disintegrated, and with it, his ticket out of town and his dreams. Suddenly, the calls from Penn State and Indiana dried up; his name vanished from the local sports pages; and Otis —who'd taken to telling everyone within earshot that his boy was going to go big-time—suddenly, Boonie and Otis and the whole goddam family had to bite the bullet and admit the truth: no Pusser was ever going to amount to a hill of shite.

Boonie, on the other hand, would always be a Pusser.

He'd put himself into the family business with a zeal since then, working long and hard to make his Pappy proud once more. It was filthy job, but it paid well, and Pussers weren't afraid to make money when there was money to be made. In fact, since he'd taken over the hard labor, sales had soared, leaving Otis to focus on public relations and his habit of stargazing through the bottom of a Jim Beam bottle.

There was, on the other hand, cousin Drew.

"Here we go, cuz," Boonie exclaimed as he approached the intersection of the road and the railroad tracks. He mumbled as he shifted the truck into low gear. Even the headlights were swallowed up by the storm, making it difficult to maneuver. He stepped on the gas and eased off the clutch, taking care not to lose the load as he rolled up onto the rails.

"Be on the lookout!" Drew moaned, his Adam's apple bobbing in his hands. He was the runt of Uncle Bud's brood, genetically a full one-eighty from the rest of the Pusser males. He was as much of a man as he would ever be at twenty years old: knock-kneed and skinny, with a chicken-bone chest and a cratered, crescent-moon face. His hair was a tangled black oil slick that dripped over his shoulders. He was dressed in a black leather jacket with little fingerless gloves, a greasy Harley T-shirt, and a plethora of biker gear, despite the fact that he didn't own a bike and couldn't ride one if he did.

Drew's favorite contact sport was a small liquid-crystal video game he played on his digital watch. It had a teeny-tiny jet that blasted a teeny-tiny city, and it played a weensy, wheedling tune every time he dropped a bomb.

The vehicle lurched once more, shaking them so violently that Drew's skull smacked against the ceiling. He grumbled, "Boonie!"

"You're fucked, puss. Hold on a second, "Boonie snarled angrily. Big knobby tires biting into rotten ties groaned and gnashed gears on the vehicle. The barrels shifted a lot, yet they stayed put.

"This place makes me fuckin' nervous," says the narrator. He fidgeted with his timepiece. It said, "Weedle eedle eee." Weedle, weedle, weedle, weedle, weedle, weedle, weedle, weedle,

"Would you be willing to remove it?" Boonie let out a bark. "Oh, my God, I despise that thing!"

"Fuck you, man," says the narrator. Drew coughed. "Dude, this is cutting-edge technology at its finest!"

weedle weedle weedle weedle

He smirked, and the last of Boonie's patience was gone. With a straight-arm, flat-hand strike to the side of Drew's head, he tagged his slender little jut-jawed profile. Drew's head shattered against the passenger-side window, and he bit down on his tongue hard enough to splatter blood.

"Ow! Bood, you're a jerk! I'm going to be dellin'! "He moaned and clutched his cheek.

"I swear to God, Drew, if you don't stuff it, I'm fuckin' leaving you here and keeping your portion of the cash."

Drew began to respond, but then abruptly and obviously changed his mind. He was quite aware, based on recent experience, that Boonie was not deceiving him.

Boonie, for one, thought it incredibly satisfying to watch Drew fold like that. It made him feel good on the inside. As a result, he chose to be gracious. "Peckerhead, here it is. I've prepared a surprise for you."

From his jacket pocket, Boonie pulled a reedy tiny joint. "That's exactly what the doctor prescribed. Start it up."

Drew sniffled as he took the doob. "Thangs," he said.

"I'll cut us a couple lines when we dump this load," Boonie remarked paternally. "In the meantime, I recommend that you warm up, because we have work to do."

Boonie slammed on the brakes and came to a shuddering halt, then gnashed the truck into reverse and humped over the tracks until the tailgate was butted up against the rail's lip. The placement was ideal. He peered out over his territory, the engine running against the cold.

The skies thundered above him, near enough for Boonie to feel it in the soles of his shoes. The night sky was pierced by a bolt of lightning. "BLOOOH-HA HA!" exclaims the narrator. In the dashboard light, Boonie cackled, his features flashing green. The windshield was splattered with the first big raindrops.

The storm has finally subsided.

The Codorus Creek has long served as a sin-eater for the Industrial Revolution: a chemical cesspool that accepted and dispensed with the excesses of the good life. Defense factories, research labs, factory farms, electroplate shops, paper mills, and landfills all decanted their waste there on a regular basis. As a result, it was already riddled with "allowed" amounts of a thousand wild-card contagions in the days before Boonie: leads, cyanides, arsenics, alkalies, chlorinated hydrocarbons, dioxins, trioxons, trichlorophenal residues, poisons, and pesticides galore.

But now, beneath the muddy surface, there lay a rusted graveyard: tons upon tons of shattered drums and rotting husks, clogging the space beneath the murky surface. The majority of the corks had long since popped, but a handful remained intact: fifty-five-gallon pockets of concentrated death, corroding the barrels from both sides and then suppurating into the slipstream.

Mutagens covered its slow surface, gently altering the molecular building blocks of everything they touched. Carcinogens nestled in its silt, drifting lazily on their way to the river and the sea. Carp and tougher garbage-eaters moved through the murky currents, their gills sucking oxygen and storing disease.

They're laying their eggs mindlessly.

Black Bridge was an industrialInstant Primordial Stew, a toxic waste dump. It's just been a century, yet it's already as rich as the brew that gave birth to life as we know it. Thousands of others like it lie inactive and asleep across the country and around the world.

It was only a matter of time until the next alarm went off.

It arrived at 3:27 a.m. that morning.

"BOMBS AWAY!" exclaims the narrator. Boonie sobbed as she rolled another down the chute.

"Bombs away!" exclaims the narrator. Drew said it again as he lowered the gate. Like a stumpy steel diving board, it jutted over the rail.

A cobalt-blue fifty-five-gallon barrel with the word DANGER painted on it rumbled down the truck bed's modest incline, then off and into the darkness below.

As gravity took over, there was a brief pause before a deep wetthwump, almost musical in tone, shattered the creek's surface like a cannonball. A plume of water rose into the air before raining down in a pelting, misty shower.

"Bull's-eye!" As he turned around, Drew cackled. "Fuckin'aye!" exclaims the narrator. He was stoned as a bastard now, kicking back behind the counter. He looked like a combination between Bazooka Joe and the Frito Bandito with his red bandanna pulled up over his nose to cut the fumes.

"Awright! Drewie is going to acquire a woody!" Boonie screamed into his paisley kerchief. "Sh*t, cuz, I knew you'd show up!"

Now the rain began to fall in earnest, wet and persistent. A summer storm slithering out from nowhere to thread through the frigid November night seemed curiously out of place, Boonie noticed. The opposing fronts collided like phantom titans. Warm rain fell on the cold ground, hissing like a whisper.

Boonie had already left his cab door open to listen to the radio. Starview 92 classic rock was playing some great vintage Allman Brothers, and Brother Greg's melancholy classic, "Midnight Rider," was blasting from the speakers.

Yes, sir, Drew smiled to himself as he nodded along with the music. We are precisely who we say we are. Man, we're the fuckin' midnight riders. It filled him with pride and made him feel really good about himself.

Drew, on the other hand, was in good spirits. It's never been better. They were drenched, but it was wonderful; a warm breeze blew around them, and the entire world shone and pulsated in rhythm with the music.

Boonie and the late great Brother Duane were trading air-guitar licks. Drew gave him a kind look while sucking on the joint through his makeshift mask. It gave him a shadow mouth with no teeth.He toked once more and sucked the scarf into his mouth, bluh bluh bluhing through the red cotton maw. Goddamn, but he could be amusing at times.

His mouth started to tingle.

The music finished, and "Riders on the Storm" began. "All right!" yelled Boonie. "Get ready! There are only thirteen days left!"

"Fuckin' aye!" exclaims the narrator. Drew shouted back, his mind wandering back to his lips. The tickle had turned into a mild burning feeling. It was most likely the drugs. To get high, Boonie would sometimes do stupid things like buy some crappy cannabis and lace it with crack, dust, or whatever he had on hand. It made you hyper-aware of your surroundings. Water trickled down his spine like rain. Like the wind howling through the trees, or the pain in his head from inhaling so many chemicals...

Drew spat, "Ech." His lips were really burning now, and he could taste it: a bitter, pungent, chemical-like sensation. It pricked the tip of his tongue with pins and tickled the roof of his mouth.

It was starting to frighten him.

"Hey, Spacely Sprocket!" says the narrator. Boonie screamed. "Are you going to help me with this?" Drew shifted his gaze to him, the barrel he was leaning against the wall.

"Boonie." In his mouth and down his neck, the name tasted terrible. And his eyes had started to itch.

"What?" says the impatient.

"Dude, I'm not feeling well." The burn intensified as he massaged his eyes.

"Ouch! Sonofabitch!" hisnostrils were now burning and the odor was becoming more intense. "Something isn't right here, guy..."

"Drew, don't get paranoid about me. I thought we were having a good time."

"Yeah, but..." says the narrator.

Directly over their heads, a thunderclap erupted in a blazing gray light. Drew could feel his nerves jangle and his heartbeat accelerate as his bones nearly flew out through his skin. "Christ!" he said, feeling dizzy for the first time.

The thunderclap died away.

However, the gray light persisted...

...and then they heard it: a crackling like ravenous flame, enormous as it welled up to cover the silence. An enraged god holds the world's largest wad of cellophane, which crinkles slowly. Static from another world is creeping in.

Coming up from the depths of the sea.

Drew shifted his gaze to Boonie. Boonie responded with an uncharacteristically blank stare. What the fuck is going on here...? Drew listened to him speak, but the sound seemed muffled. The barrel slid from his fingers and landed on its side on the truck bed. Drew winced, rather than hearing it, he felt it.

And the booming drone remained, becoming increasingly liquid rather than static as he listened. He turned toward it, wobbling for the gate, his head muzzy and his body numb from the power. Between his thrumming fingertips, the roach slipped unnoticed.

Drew stood on the ledge, staring out over the edge.

14

At the dreadful source of the noise.

The fish were attempting to escape the water. There was simply no other way to put it. They were actually flinging themselves into the air, leaping and writhing in a last-ditch attempt to defy gravity. As if they were trying to evolve on their own, into birds that could fly away to heaven, or into anything else that might be able to escape and survive.

There isn't one.

There's no way.

As the water beneath them began to bubble and swirl, he looked in dread. The gray light flickered for a moment, then faded to black.

Boonie screamed from behind him.

Drew turned just in time to see the drum approaching him, speeding up as it approached the edge. It was the one who had escaped his cousin's grasp, but it wasn't the only one who had moved.

The remaining dozen barrels rocked and shuddered on their bases, making the entire back of the truck a flurry of nervous action. It was as if something had come to life within them.

As if that item yearned to be free.

Drew just managed to avoid the drum as it slammed past him and disappeared over the cliff. A lengthy, astonishingly pregnant moment of thunderous quiet followed.

The drum then shattered the surface, like sperm digging into an egg.

As a result, the new world was born.

Born of poison and raised in poison, it arose as a raw creation miracle, a scorching black cry of life and death entwined and converted to some third new alternative anguish blip with an echoing tail so long. It seemed to go on forever, but now the dog's tail was wagging, dredging up silt and sewage and bursting metal eggshell skins in a riotous shrapnel dance of power surging self-aware mass assassinating shape infesting polluting corrupting in hideous birthday celebration it rose already killing and stared into the face of its maker.

When the tremendous liquid blowback erupted, Drew was less than six feet away from the rail: a solid pillar of displaced fluid that flew from the creek to the pinnacle of Black Bridge in a fraction of a second. It loomed over him and lingered there, shattering physics and dismantling logic.

Assembling into shape.

The gigantic greasy serpent loomed, not freeze-framed or immobile, but undulating like a wind funnel. It did not appear to be real against the black sky, yet he could sense the incredible life-shredding charge of its presence vibrating in the air. It caused every hair on his body to stand on end in sheer horror.

Then the lightning struck, completely liberating him from his sanity. He could see the things that suffered and whirled within it all too vividly in the light. The rusty struts and rotten shells of the barrels were visible: skeletal and clawed. Its blood and spirit were multicolored Rorschach poisons, which could be seen.

Hundreds of fish could be seen: not dead, but no longer alive.

They were all staring at each other. At him, to be precise.

Seeing things through new eyes...

Then the lightning faded, and the black wall came upon him before he could scream.

In the split second before the truck hit, Boonie jumped off the side. When many tons went WHOOOM and splashed on its bed, he was still in the air. He couldn't tell what had happened to Drew because he couldn't see him. He didn't need to see to realize he couldn't do anything.

Boonie was a big guy who fell rapidly. He hadn't got enough time to plan his route. The train lines rushed up to meet him, head-on and at an alarming speed.

He raised his arms and tucked his body in tight enough to keep his neck from snapping. All he got was a broken collarbone and, on the second bounce, some teeth and lip, which melted into a wet bone-shard buckshot hail that suffocated him as he rolled, came up, and automatically assessed the situation.

Except for the steam curling off the truck's exterior, there was no movement from the truck. The door remained open, the cab remained empty, and the headlights continued to beam. Toad Road and escape waited beyond the truck; the other path only continued deeper into the Black Bridge forests. He could drive at a far faster rate than he could run.

That was pretty much the end of it. Boonie jumped into the cab, one eye on the railroad ties and the other on the forty-foot monsters. The air was filled with a harsh static crackle that grew louder as he got closer. It wasn't the stream, therefore it couldn't have been shit.

When he got into the driver's seat, he realized it was the radio. Starview 92 had devolved into a deafening hiss. This is a bad sign. He snatched up the stick and slammed it into the gears. There was no action. He stomped on the gas and passed out.

"GOD DAMN IT!" exclaims the narrator. Grabbing the keys and hammering the ignition, he yelled. "Let's go...!"

He observed the rivulets running over the windscreen at that point. Not at all. Across: a lateral, spider-webbing motion, as if the cab were gripped by a hundred liquid tentacles. As the glass began to steam, he stood dumbfounded and slack-jawed. The liquid pressed against the pane and squeezed impossibly.

Boonie swooped in for the passenger seat, clutching the handle. The safety glass shone brightly all around him. He slammed the door open and began to flee...

...as a blinding, razoredspray blew in through the windows...

...and then he was out the door, racing for his life, a thousand small shrapnel barbs lodged in his face, hands, and feet. His neck, back, and legs tripped on a tie and knocked him down, all 247 pounds of him, crying in agony as his scar-pitted Frankenstein's former right knee slammed the cold steel rail...

...but he couldn't remain down or the game would be finished, so he pushed himself back to his feet and hobbled as hard as he could. Ignoring the anguish, ignoring the tingle that evolved into a horrible burn in his eyes, the left eye hurting sharply, wet, and bleeding from within...

As he staggered in puddles of primal rain, he continued to run, trading the rails for Toad Road muck, screaming out pleas to lovely baby Jesus.

He's fleeing from the devil he keeps in his back pocket.

He ran until he collapsed...

Chapter Two

The undulating length of God's kingdom that was Paradise, Pennsylvania was decorated with 188 thousand souls. With the craggy hump of the Appalachian foothills reaching across the west and the huge rocky expanse of the Susquehanna River to the east, it was slightly over 900 square miles of spacious, magnificent terrain.

Paradise was the natural nerve hub for trucks of all kinds because it was the nexus point of the region's principal east/west and north/south highways. Big tractors rumbled in and out all the time, transporting the necessities of life east to Philadelphia and New York. South to Baltimore and Washington; north to Harrisburg and Allentown; and west to Pittsburgh and the Ohioan heartlands beyond, through the turnpike.

The outside townships were largely made up of farms, factories, and forest area, lush hills and hollows thinly populated and broken up by strip malls and lonely one-horse hamlets that accounted for maybe 37,000.

Around seventy-three thousand people live in the industrial parks. which in turn gave way to wave after wave of densely packed, self-replicating suburbia: houses and lawns, As the neighborhoods topped the hills and entered the valley that defined the city proper, they shrank in size. They crammed in tighter and tighter until the lawns dissolved into puddle-sized areas or vanished completely.

On the south side of town, the City Reservoir was the highest elevation and the location of the Paradise Water Company's large standing pools. A panorama unfolded before you if you stood on the crest of the hill and gazed out over the valley: lights glittering in the deep blue predawn stillness, a thoroughly American picture-postcard jumble of church steeples and smokestacks, homes and factories, parks and schools.

There were 78 thousand people living and dreaming there, on small one-way streets and shady tree-lined boulevards. College Avenue's decaying tarpaper shanties and charming Cape Cods; Market Square townhouses and lush Georgian abodes of Linden Boulevard's attractively refurbished Market Square townhouses and lush Georgian abodes.

One hundred and eighty-eight thousand pulses pounded through the night, ticking off the moments of a lifetime, from the affluent palatial mansions of Wyndham Hills to the paper-thin walls of the Paradise Rescue Mission—and everywhere in between.

The cost of living in Paradise was cheap, and the unemployment rate was a few tenths of a percentage point lower than the national average. In the previous thirty years, the black and Hispanic communities—and, more lately, the Asian community—have enjoyed consistent expansion. Despite all of this, as well as a robust, rich Jewish population, there has been a very small Asian inflow. The same Dutch-German hands that had wrested this area from the Indians now held the reins of local administration and industry.

This was a land where faschnachts and pig roasts coexisted with tractor pulls and trailer parks, country clubs and county fairs, and women' invitational golf tournaments. Paradise County, like much of the noncosmopolitan East, was known for its stodginess and slow-moving aversion to change, a trait shared by both the high and lower classes.

However, once you got passed their origins, it was television that truly created and defined their culture: from CBN to MTV, PBS to HBO, with network news, halftime programs, and prime-time fodder dominionover everything.

In a nutshell, that was America.

And, like the rest of America, Paradise slept: until the early hours of Sunday morning. One hundred and eighty-eight thousand people lay down in lonely slumber across the city and county, subconsciously intertwined.

And not a single one of them saw it coming.

Chapter Three

Gwen awoke with the phantom remnants of REM-stage sleep still hanging to her thoughts like a shroud when she opened her eyes.

Black birds swooped and soared in a figure-eight pattern in the dream, thousands of them, their iridescent wings and piercing cries filling the sky.

Over and over...

Gwen felt a peculiar sense of dislocation as the image faded, fading like morning fog and leaving her with a strange sense of consciousness arriving a split second before identity. She had no idea who, where, or what she was for a brief moment.

She was only that.

Alive and well.

Here.

It was a strange sensation, unsettling but not completely awful. She let it soak in for a few moments, allowing it to color her perceptions without bias or prejudice.

She felt a jolt inside her.

And it all came back to me.

Gwen Taylor is my name. I'm a thirty-year-old woman. I'm in my room, in my house, in my bed.

It kicked once more, this time with a small solid thump from deep within.

She added, "And I'm expecting a baby."

A puff of subconscious synaptic flotsam was vaporized by thought, and the dislocation vanished. Gwen stretched and yawned in the large brass bed. Her sleep-tossed ash-blond hair flowed across the pillow, and the faintest trace of smile crinkles delicately framed her pure gray eyes.

She was a strikingly lovely woman, though you'd never get her to agree with that recently: nine months in, she resembled an anaconda with a hippo wedged in its digestive tube. To put it another way, she solely believed the wordsdingo ugly to accurately represent her self-image, and there was nothing Gary or anybody else could say to convince her otherwise.

On the other side, she felt fairly well today: warm, happy, and loved, with only a smidgeon of nausea to keep things grounded. On Thursday, the baby had dropped, its head settling into her pelvis in preparation for the final stretch. It relieved some of the strain, making her feel a bit less bloated and ungainly, and most definitely increased her excitement.

She muttered to the growing form inside her, "Won't be long now." "You're going to enjoy yourselves here."

She peered out from beneath the blankets, imagining herself lounging all day. From her vantage point, it was a dreary morning; the old casement windows rattled as the wind tried to get in; a stray ray of predawn light shined coldly through the gap in the curtains, highlighting the dust motes swirling in the air.

The heat was recirculated by the ceiling fan, which swung lazily overhead. The house was a three-story frame residence located 10 miles north of town on Starview Road in East Manchester township. It was almost a century old and had been meticulously restored by Gary and Gwen until it exuded warmth, character, and a distinct sense of home.

Their room was a little drafty, but it was bigger now that Gary had taken through the back wall, decreasing the number of available bedrooms in the old farmhouse from four to three while greatly expanding the area.

After all, a guest room and a nursery are all we really need, she reasoned, her hands moving up over the bulk of her tummy. This is a one-time event.

The baby kicked once more.

Gwen shifted her gaze to Gary, who was still sleeping beside her, his body hidden beneath a mountain of rumpled down. "Gary," she said quietly. He shifted in his sleep and muttered something incomprehensible into his pillow. She tickled him from behind the cover. "Gary?"

Gary groaned and shifted in his sleep, but he didn't wake up. She took a breath and just stared at her man.

To those who knew him, it was difficult to believe Gary Taylor was thirty-seven years old; based on his energy level alone, he appeared to be at least a dozen years younger. However, she could see his years and all the hardship he'd been under carved in the rugged lines of his face when he was at ease like this—with his personality temporarily on hold.

Gary was a tall, lean lupine man with a tough fighter's visage softened by lovely eyes and a floppy paintbrush mustache. His hair was black and thick, with a widow's peak high on his forehead and a faint silvering around the temples. The pillow side stayed smushed when he rolled toward her, sticking up like a tar baby's mop.

Gwen grinned and squeezed him from beneath the covers. She joked, "Gary, you 'wake?"

With one eye open, he gave her a cold stare.

"Spike kicked," she murmured, a beautiful smile on her face. "Three times," says the narrator.

Gary blinked once and then again. He was waiting for enough blood to flow through his brain for him to be able to speak. He'd been up late the night before, summoned to the station at the last minute by yet another technical issue that Bob the Knob couldn't solve. He muttered, "Mmm." "Mmph."

"He stated he wanted to see his grandfather," Gwen explained.

"Mmph," Gary said again, his head buried in the cushion. "He doesn't let me sleep if he doesn't let me sleep."

Gwen remarked slyly, disregarding him, "He's not the only one." Hormones spiked in the ninth month, for no apparent reason; they plucked and teased her erogenous zones like phantom limbs' eerie murmurs.

It wasn't quite arousal; at this point, she often doubted that she'd ever feel truly turned on—in the traditional sense—again. Instead, she had a strong desire to be made attractive in order to appease her unfounded fears and be reassured, through physical contact, that she wasn'treally too repulsive to live, and that Gary could still be able to love her.

She snatched a handful of excellent thick morning boner from between Gary's legs. Gary, on the other hand, moaned and smiled. Evidently, there is no rest for the wicked. He stared at his wife with hazy eyes, who smiled and worked him beneath the sheets. "I swear, you're incorrigible," he hissed throatily. She chuckled slyly, a guttural chuckle.

Gary put his hand on her belly and felt the strong round firmness of her belly, as well as the fullness of her breasts, which had grown to half their regular size throughout the pregnancy. He gazed at her; she was the most gorgeous creature he'd ever seen, sleepy-eyed, big-bellied, and disheveled.

He said, "Mornin', mother."

"Mmmmm," Gwen said. "I adore you."

He said, "I love you back." Gary daubed Gwen with morning-mouth kisses, feeling the liquid smoothness of her lips and tasting the familiar musky sweetness of her neck as she leaned forward a little.

Gary's attitude toward sex these days was the kinder, gentler counterpart of Gwen's. He didn't feel arousal in the same way: he felt extremely protective and deeply loving toward her, rather than turned on. After all, she was his lady love, and the only animal who even came close to matching his emotions was about to poot forth from her loins.

He could love them both right now with a single simple gesture, and give Gwen the reassurance she so sorely needed.

It doesn't get much more convenient than that.

As she spooned his cock against her rear and guided him between her legs, he murmured, "Anything special planned today?"

"Mmmm," she replied, her attention diverted for a time. "Remember picking up Micki at eleven?"

He moaned, "Oh, yeah." "Micki." Whoa, whoa, whoa, whoa, whoa, whoa, Tofu, sandalwood, crystals, and pentacles flashed in his mind. "How long will she be here?"

"Until the baby is born, and I'm back on my feet," Gwen said, expecting the opposition. Gary mumbled something. That meant cannabis walks, witchy rituals, and odd diets on the West Coast for at least six weeks. If history is any guide, there will very certainly be more.

"It'll be healthy for the kid," she explained as she shifted into a more comfortable position. "Besides, we have the book to finish... "

Gary groaned again as he shoved his face against her. Gwen took it in stride, lifting one leg and angling her hips. As the gates parted and Gary slipped home, her pelvis spread for the passage, her lips moist and full.

They settled on a languid, sensual beat of heat, love, and life, and the fight was over before it really began.

And thus another Sunday in Paradise began.

Chapter four

At half past six, the first light fell on Dark Hollow Road, cutting through Windsor Township's scraggly woods, dividing the night into tiny strips of shade. The storm had faded to mist and memory, but the night had begun to fade as well. It was replaced by obnoxious, cloud-refracted sunlight, which was unseasonably warm and difficult to look at.

But, on the other hand, everything was now painful.

He was a huge dying man who couldn't go much further. Every trembling, agonizing step forward was a supreme exercise of determination. He'd been driving south down Hellam's rural roads in this manner for hours.

He didn't have complete control over his will.

He came to a halt at the final curve, swinging grotesquely swelled. The Flinchbaugh place spread out in front of him like a garish, white-trash Disneyland; it was all that stood between him and his house. Eb Flinchbaugh's immaculate lawn was crammed with lawn ornaments: concrete jockey and leprechaun features trapped in lifeless smiles, small

Dutch girl's eyes looking sightlessly through him as he walked by.

Artificial flamingos and deer were grouped around the focal point: a functional fountain that burbled nonstop, relaxing his ears. The temptation to simply lie down among them and rest—possibly indefinitely—was strong.

He couldn't stand by and let it happen.

Not with him so close.

He plunged into the hollow one shivering, stumbling step at a time. The rust-hued sheen of the yard below was like a beacon for Boonie's own finish line in the bad-news relay race.

I'm calling him to come home.

Otis Pusser arrived at the gate at 7:00 p.m., slouching beneath the peeling vinyl top of his 1979 Buick Skylark. He leaned into the horn, his huge palm pressing down so hard on the wheel rim that it felt like it was about to fall off.

"GODDAMMIT! BONUS! "He screamed. "THIS GODDAMNED GATE MUST BE OPENED!"

Like a buttfucked sow, the horn lowed. DamDog and Coonie joined in behind the gate, their raggedy junkyard yowls adding to the din. They were mutts, scrawny-assed and ruthless to a fault, born to be vicious and kept that way. Coon jumped all fours into the air and snapped at the chain link while watching, then came down on DamDog and was bitten as a result. The air was thick with fur, dog feces, and dust.

He mumbled, shaking his head and honking again, "Stupid stupid creatures."

He didn't have any keys; he just didn't want to get out of bed. Otis weighed in at a smidgeon over 350 pounds, the most of which was hard fat and body odor. His nose was a lively rococo mural of crimson capillary anguish, and his features were large-pored and leathery—the wages of a life of hard labor. Between his thighs was a Big Gulp cup filled three-to-one with coffee and Wild Turkey.

Otis looked up, perplexed. PUSSER'S SCRAP & SALVAGE was written on a pocked metal sign over the gate. It was his bread and butter, his legacy, and his lifeline.

Which explained why Otis was so irritated in the first place. Where was his bad-boy son when he was all dressed up and ready to go? The little shit is probably stone-drunk and napping.

Otis gave the horn one last blat, but it was in vain. "Some balls will roll," he mumbled, before flinging open the door and squeezing through the opening. Waddling over to unlock the gate took a minute, and he swung it back, hitting the dogs in the process. DamDog yipped and scurried away from Coon.

"Bitch! Get the hell out of here!" Returning to the car, Otis barked. As he revved the engine and drove into Pusserland proper, the hounds scattered.

It was a little more than three acres of rusting garbage, the cannibalized remains of the American dream. Automobiles that have been abandoned. Refrigerators that have been abandoned. Air conditioners and water heaters that have been abandoned. There was a lot of simply plain garbage that passed through Otis' hands on its route to oblivion.

Otis had a keen sense of value and a vast network of contacts. He could remove the copper from a Kool King's teeth faster than akapo could, and he knew exactly who to sell it to. It was a present.

He smiled as he remembered the load from the night before. Not bad for a single evening's labor. Twenty-five drums at $40 each, for a total of $1,500 for the basic magic trick of making someone else's problem vanish. Otis was an alchemical endstop in society's digestive tract, sucking up the last ounce of worth and turning garbage into gold.

Pusser's was the dungheap at the end of the line in the larger scheme of things.

And Otis reigned supreme over Turd Mountain.

He drove down the main road to the trailer, a forty-foot Airstream that served as both an office and a bachelor home for Boonie. Even though the truck was gone, Otis parked next to it and got out, noting that the lights in the trailer were still on. He was thinking about how he was going to run up the goddamnedelectric bill once more. Today was going to be a day of major buttkicking.

With fatherly, corporate, and intoxicated wrath, he stormed toward the trailer door. He discovered it unlocked and ajar, much to his dismay. In the pale blue dawn, a small sliver of gold light squirted out the crack.

He slammed his way into the room, ready to pounce.

Then it came to an abrupt halt.

The trailer's interior was claustrophobic, smelled of spilled beer and gym socks, and stuffed with junk furniture and old pornographic magazines. Another odor lingered in the closed, dark chamber, strong, chemical, and overpowering.

The youngster was huddled in front of a mirror placed on the battered steel desk that served as the office's delineation. For illumination, a gooseneck lamp was coiled up.

Boonie whirled as if caught jerking off when the door flung open, yet his expression revealed far less surprise than anguish. When his father burst in, he had been wailing.

"Jesus H. Christ," Otis murmured, staring dumbfounded at his son's shambles.

"Pa..." says the narrator. Boonie sobbed as she stuffed psychic ice chunks down Otis' spine.

In one hand, he held a pair of bloody tweezers, and in the other, a gore-smeared cloth. Like a gruesome show from Van Scoy's Diamond Mine, a pile of glass cubes glistened before him. The other half of the reward was still lodged in Boonie's face.

The cleansed side was raw, nearly abscessed; the lacerations had swelled up, resulting in clusters of tiny open sores, like craters on his alien face, nose, and forehead terrain.

On the table was an uncorked bottle of hydrogen peroxide. Boonie grasped it with swollen fingers and dipped the rag in the liquid, then dabbed his damaged right cheek with it.

It fizzed loudly and spewed pinkish froth; Boonie screamed and raised one clawed hand to hover an inch away from the enraged surface. His eyes were bloodshot and watery orbs when he peered up at Otis. "I messed up, Pa. Pa, I messed up big time..."

As Boonie confessed, Otis listened. It took two minutes to complete. Otis didn't trust half of what his child said since he was stoned, but the other half more than made up for it.

Otis had more than enough time to visualize his kingdom falling beneath his feet after two sweeps of the second hand.

Otis waited till Boonie was finished before getting the facts straight.

Then he kicked him in the shins.

First and foremost.

Chapter five

Harold Leonard laughed and said, "You're joking."

On his brow was a thin sheen of really cold sweat. It hadn't been there for a long time. He'd just piled Marge and their six wonderful children into the Arrow, ready to attend to another Sunday church in style. Following a brief time of Christian fellowship, the Bob's Big Boy buffet was served. Although it was a little chilly for golf, Harold was a true believer. He'd be back in time for the Eagles game after a quick nine holes at the club.

He'd figured it out a minute before.

That minute had passed inexorably.

The person on the other end of the line sounded inebriated, irritable, and out of breath. It informed him that it wasn't a prank and then continued to rattle off a long list of extremely nasty details. Every single one of them fanned the flame of fear that had taken root in his lungs, peeing fire into his scrawny gut.

Harold Leonard owned and operated Paradise Garbage Disposal, the largest legal waste disposal plant in the area. The local industrial community had come to him with its dirty diapers for the past fifteen years, paying him handsomely to clean them up or, at the very least, keep them somewhere inoffensive and secure.

The good news was that business was booming, and waste was something we never ran short of. Unfortunately, there was far too much of it. Even with the most cutting-edge equipment he could afford, he could only process a fraction of what he was given. Every hour, every day, every month, and every year.

That's where Harold's operation teetered on the edge of breaking the law.

Harold Leonard was a pickle in the middle in every sense of the word: middle-aged, middle-class. In the professional world, he commanded a level of respect that he rarely received in his personal life. He was the overweight kid who always got two for flinching, liver-lipped, beak-nosed, and weasel-eyed, and the last man you'd pick for your squad in school.

He was flinching now, there was no doubt about it. In his porcine hand, the phone's receiver was slippery. "Don't do something dumb," he grumbled to himself. "We'll figure it out."

The voice on the other phone screamed, "You're goddam right, we'll work this out." "I'm curious as to what you're going to do regarding my boys."

Harold was at a loss for words. For obvious reasons, the hospital was closed. His mind raced, looking for backup plans that didn't exist. "Take a look," he said. "I need to speak with a few folks. Have you told anyone else about it yet?"

"Are you deafeningly deafeningly deafening

He silently praised God, and his brain began to work at that very instant. Maybe it had something to do with the power of prayer. "All right, pay attention," he said. "First and foremost, I'd like you to call the cops."

"That's right! You're fucked!"

"Will you pay attention to me?" Harold pressed harder this time. He was back in his element, weaseling in real time and thinking quickly. "Inform them that you have just arrived and that the truck has been taken. Last night, most likely."

He made a colorful noise of comprehension to the moron with whom he was speaking. Harold pressed on, redeemed in his own eyes."If they find it, that'll cover you, and it'll allow us some time to figure this out."

"Okay. That appeals to me..."

"Keep your big mouth shut for the sake of Christ. Don't say anything to anyone until I return your call."

Leonard threw the phone down, abruptly interrupting their conversation. Then he just stood there, shaking for a long, horrible minute, trying valiantly to calm himself. His heart slammed into his temples as his ulcer bubbled like a gastric Jacuzzi.

"Everything's going to be alright," he reminded himself, despite his best efforts not to believe it. "All I have to do now is inform Blake. He'll figure it out..."

Outside, Marge or one of the kids banged on the horn, "Shave and a Haircut."

It jolted him out of his trance and made him crave their warmth and company. He reassured himself, "I'm not a bad guy."

It's difficult for me to believe it.

I'm not like that...

Then Harold Leonard put on his coat and hat, locked the door to his comfortable little house in Haines Acres, and went through the yard of his tucked-away slice of suburban paradise.

And he went to worship with his lovely family.

He will be buried in the church of his choice.

Chapter Six

The legions of God's faithful were off and running by a quarter after eleven on a Sunday morning.

Whatever else one may say about Paradise County residents, Deitz observed that they were big on Sunday services. There were certainly no shortage of God-anointed service stations with eighty-seven buildings of worship within the city limits alone, representing twenty-eight Christian faiths. The virtuous deployed as the wicked slept in, gathering en masse to their various personal savior pit spots.

The children of God made their holy presence known from the Mennonite farms at the county's edge to the African Episcopal Church downtown. They practically owned the roads between the hours of 9 a.m. and noon: station wagons crammed with Baptists, Brethren, and Bible Fellows; drive-thru windows dispensed Sausage and Egg McMuffins by the truckload to Methodists and Mormons alike; and gas stations supplying Catholics, Christian Scientists, Seventh-Day Adventists, and Assemblymen of God.

Austin Deitz stood in the back of the Mt. Rose Amoco Shop 'N' Go, near the intersection of Route 24 and Mt. Rose Road. Rose Avenue is located at the eastern valley's mouth. While he waited for Jennie to return, he was perusing the Yummy Potato Chip snack rack.

She'd vanished five minutes ago inside the Employees Only door. As shop manager, she'd been dragged from her bed and summoned to deal with the latest crisis: some loser named Ozzie who'd called in ill with tickets to the Eagles game at the last minute.

Ozzie's current status as a jobless person was little consolation. Ozzie's power to cancel their Sunday plans was the only thing that piqued his attention. After all, it was a once-in-a-lifetime event.

They're celebrating their fourth—count 'em, fourth—anniversary.

Deitz smiled as he reflected on their four weeks together. Oh, my God. That's over a month's worth of work! Someone should notify the media!

It's been almost a month since I've been genuinely joyful.

Austin Deitz, a tall gangly man with knobby calloused hands and a face like a young Abe Lincoln's, was a month shy of forty. He had the same piercing dark eyes and stern, gaunt hollows in his cheekbones, as well as the same cowlicked hair shock and horsey overbite. The only things he needed were a beard and a gunshot hole, neither of which he was eager to acquire.

Jennie didn't seem to mind that he wasn't quite what he'd call a love machine. She'd changed his mind about a number of things since their eyes met over the barbecue chicken pit at the Stoverstown Fire Company's Fall Festival.

Jennie Quirez was little and slim, with a broad but delicate face framed by warm mahogany hair and finished off by the clearest, most beautiful deep brown eyes he'd ever seen. She was probably in her late twenties or early thirties—Deitz hadn't asked yet, but he didn't think she'd mind—far enough along for her rich tan complexion to take on the supple, slightly leathery etch of time. There could not have been a more perfect wish-fulfillment fantasy for a kid who grew up thinking Heinlein and Bradbury were gods than a girl who understood what it meant to grok in fullness, or who could appreciate both the strange peace and melancholic beauty of a book like The Martian Chronicles and the icy, hardwired edginess of Gibson'sNeuromancer.

But the science fiction she adored was intrinsically hopeful, just like her. She loved to believe that there were clever, caring, and kind creatures out there somewhere, and that one day we'd evolve sufficiently to join them among the stars.

Furthermore, she liked to encourage those qualities in people on Earth for what she thought were fairly obvious reasons: a) to help us evolve a little bit faster; b) because, quite simply, life was better when people were treated well; and c) because the odds were good that, given her current career trajectory, she'd never actually make it into space.

He convinced himself that she'd find someone to work for her. Just have a little faith in yourself. The Baltimore Aquarium and the Inner Harbor are on your itinerary, followed by supper at Dobson's and a stay at the Hunt Valley Inn. To put it another way, you can't fail.

Continue to play your cards correctly. Also, please pray for a miracle.

Today could be the most important day of your life.

It was, of course, correct. Or, at the very least, it may be. Every Sunday since he'd met Jennie had been better than the one before. It was the first time Deitz had gotten so close to someone so rapidly in what seemed like an eternity.

It felt a little like falling in love.

That, in and of itself, was nothing short of a miracle.

Meanwhile, Deitz wandered aimlessly through the aisles, waiting. There wasn't a single nontoxic food unit in the entire goddam store—not Jennie's fault; she was a manager, not a buyer—but that didn't stop a dozen customers from filling up on nutritionally deficient, oversalted, or sugar-laden treats. Deitz stood there watching them compare poisons in a frantic attempt to divert his attention away from his growing fear.

He looked down at the data pager tucked into his belt, its tiny power light flashing brightly all the time. What if something goes wrong? As he watched Dobson's and the Hunt Valley Inn sprout wings and soar away without them, he sighed.

The beeper kept alert while remaining blissfully silent.

Okay, then, he reasoned. What if she is unable to locate a substitute...?

"Now," he said, interrupting himself. "Remember what you said? Nothing affects you these days. You're the happiest man on the face of the planet."

But there were other things that were much easier stated than done.

Behind the counter, a drab-eyed young lady sat on a stool. As she rung up a PTL housewife with a stack of fudge brownies stacked like poker chips in front of her, she shoved a Tastykake into her lips. Pat, read the girl's cheesy plastic name tag. Hi! Pat is my name.

Pat's swollen fishbelly features seemed to whiten and mysteriously morph in the flat, bright glare, the rounded shoulders and rippling buttocks merging into the stool, erasing her identity totally, until she became one vast, pallid, lumpen pyramid of consumption incarnate.

Deitz imagined her as a horrible Eating Machine, the cake disappearing down her champing jaws like a log feeding into a tree shredder for that little period of fantasy.

The fact that it wasn't just any Tastykake, but aKreme-Filled Krummy Kake, only added to the fun. Pat would get her daily adult requirements of mono-calcium phosphate, mono and diglycerides, calcium lactate, and propylene glycol monostearate in addition to everything else. Just to name a few.

Breakfast that is both complete and balanced.

For the sake of a decrepit and dying race.

"Blech," he grumbled as he averted his gaze.

He knew it was impolite to gaze, but he couldn't stop himself. It was difficult to comprehend that people could be so clueless. It had been a long time since he'd indulged in such blissful ignorance.

It was difficult to remain unspoiled in a world of nonsense, but Austin Deitz did his best. BHA and BHT, propyl gallate, and yellow 5 were all on his no-no list, which included everything from Snickers bars to Starburst fruit chews. He avoided sodium benzoate at all costs, which effectively ruled out nearly every drink in the institution, from orange drink to iced tea to Mountain Dew. He didn't want to think about the secret ingredients on their lunch meat subs and ballpark franks that were kept unlabeled.

The folks at Yummy Potato Chips were a different story: a little business that created a name for itself by using less preservatives than their national competitors. To indicate salt 'n' vinegar or bring out the zing in those "natural smoke tastes," they used the same old bag of tricks: a little calcium silicate, monosodium glutamate, sodium acetate, and fumaric acid.

Which pretty much left him with the unsalted peanuts and imported mountain spring water, both packaged in nonrecyclable plastic that was destined to outlast his greatgrandchildren's grandchildren. That is, assuming that he everhad kids.

That was totally out of the question.

And it was here that he was continuously compelled to defend himself: from his parents, the women he loved, and the boys he grew up with who wanted to lead him toward a Normal Life. It wasn't that Deitz was this irrational, paranoid jerk who didn't like Christians, snack cakes, or children. The reality was both easier and more difficult to accept.

Austin Deitz was a member of the Hazardous Materials unit.

He'd seen far too much.

Normally, HazMat was the responsibility of a younger guy, but Deitz saw it as his purpose and the meaning of his existence. Years earlier, he had started out as an ordinary firefighter who wanted to save lives and be challenged by nature's often terrible whims. The transition to HazMat was gradual but inevitable, like being smashed by a train that took ten years to arrive. Despite this, he never felt he had a choice.

Because if you were lucky enough to witness the planet's gradual, subtle poisoning, you did everything you could to stop it. You did what you could, even if it wasn't enough— even if nothing could ever be enough—because what else could you do?

There was no such thing as not knowing once you knew.

There was no going back once you'd seen.

The drift, like its price, was unavoidable. He'd lost two spouses, a lot of his peace of mind, and most of his hope for the future as a result of it. Deitz felt like he was fighting for survival against our own folly on the savage front lines of humanity's final struggle.

He truly believed he'd seen everything, and in some ways he had. However, the majority of people had not seen it, smelled it, or had their faces ground in it like he had. And, hopefully, they never will.

That's why they were still able to eat and drink this garbage. That was the only way they could continue to have children. They grasped the concept intellectually—if they thought about it at all—but they lacked emotional or experiential connection.

They didn't realize it until it was too late.

And it seems that this was the deciding factor...

Jennie's sneakers slapped the floors behind him as theEMPLOYEES ONLY door finally slid open. He half-turned toward her and felt her arms snake around his waist, squeezing him like a serpent. She pecked him on the back of the neck and moaned, "Mmmmm." It was a stretch for me at five feet four inches. "Exciting news."

"Tell me." He smiled down at her as he twisted in her arms.

""I contacted everyone on the list at least a dozen times before I eventually got through to Babs," she said. She claims, however, that she will be able to arrive at three o'clock."

"Three?" Deitz bemoaned, his smile fading and his displeasure audible in his voice. The Aquarium closed at five o'clock, leaving them with little over an hour to take in the sights after an hour to get down and another twenty minutes to park...

"I'm sorry," she responded emphatically. "That's the best I can do. If you don't want to take a rain check or..."

"Nuh-uh-uh. There's no way." He attempted to send his smile all the way down to her toes, but he couldn't. "I'm afraid I'll have to be firm on this subject."

"All right," she replied, smiling as brightly as she could. "Then don't be frightened. We're going to have a great time."

She added another grip and a smile to the vow, and dammit if he didn't believe her. There was something about her that blew through every gap in his defenses like a spring breeze through the rusted armor around his soul.

Deitz was convinced after just one look at her.

"This power must only be utilized for good," he muttered low in his voice.

She burst out laughing. "Are you going to be here at three?"

"At the very least."

"Absolutely." She looked at him with wide pleading black velvet eyes. "Remember, you're my ride?"

"Mmm-hmmm." They kissed in hushed tones, as if they didn't want God's small customers to complain. "Before three o'clock, I'll be here."

"But not too soon... "

"I'll be here in two minutes and three seconds." It was a solemn, deadpan vow. "I swear with my whole heart."

"We've reached an agreement." Jennie grinned and disengaged, then slid behind the counter across the frantic room. Deitz kept an eye on her as she walked past the microwave and lunch meats, which were a constant source of nitrates and low-level radiation.

He overheard Jennie say, "Thank you so much for staying on, Patty." "I apologise profusely."

"S'okay." Patty grinned, her drab expression lightening a little. "It's not like it's entirely your fault."

Pat the Eating Machine then magically turned back into a real flesh-and-blood human being.

Pat became Patty, a fatigued girl who'd deliberately, responsibly stayed an hour and a half past her typical graveyard shift, all because of some irresponsible jerkoff named Ozzie, thanks to Jennie's charity. Pat, the dreadful

Monster From Hell, transformed into Patty, a sweet and relieved young woman who could finally return home.

As she turned over the keys to Jennie, who'd left breakfast in bed and a half-read Sunday Baltimore Sun to come in and save the day, Deitz observed Patty's unashamed appreciation. And who hadn't complained, sulked, or whined about it, but had instead taken it all in stride.

Yes, he agreed. There's no doubt about that. Jennie Quirez has the potential to completely transform your outlook on life...

The entrance door swung open. He was unconcerned about it. From halfway across the room, his gaze was drawn to Jennie's lips, which were puckering up for his benefit. He smiled as he noticed a flurry of black-and-white activity in his peripheral vision.

It had caught him off guard. He began to turn. A tangle of bone-white hair framed a pale, broad, deathlike face. It belonged to a punk-rock adolescent with scorching emerald eyes and darkly etched thin lips.

She was dressed totally in black, from her black blouse to her black leggings to her clunky black shitkicker jump boots. He hadn't recognized how small she was at first: her hair gave her an easy five inches of height, putting her eye level with Deitz's breastbone. Her close-shaved temples had a little downy stubble. The stubble was also white.

Deitz realized he was gazing, jerked his gaze away, and wasn't surprised to see that everyone else was doing the same. She didn't appear to be on her way to church on a Sunday. As she walked across the room, her face drowsy from an unsatisfied urge for sleep, she drew every look in the room with her. Maybe it's the medications. Or both, perhaps.

He turned to face Jennie, who was beaming. Check her out, Jennie said, her words drawn out for clarity's sake. She's a ree-lee oddball. Deitz smiled and nodded before turning back to watch the female approach him.

She came to a halt at the coffee shop and proceeded to fill a 32-ounce Big Gulp with steaming java. He thought to himself, "Yikes." She's not going to church, which is a good thing. She'd be bouncing up and down in the pews. He kept a low profile as she poured roughly four packets of sugar into the cup and swirled it around before reaching for the nondairy creamer units.

She then paused to read the label, much to his surprise.

Deitz was taken aback. For a little while, even his internal monologue ceased to exist. In the entire time he'd been waiting, not a single person had given a second thought to what they were putting in their mouths. It surprised him, but it pleased him that the black sheep would be the only one who knew.

For a brief while, he considered the possibility that she was simply reading the brand name. However, this is not the case. Her lips silently moved in conjunction with the list of components ribboned around the label's edge as she twisted the thing slowly between her fingers, like a volume knob: Water, salt, and partly hydrogenated soybean oil are among the ingredients...

He couldn't contain himself any longer as she smiled and fumbled to pronounce sodium stearoyl lactylate.

He took a step closer and exclaimed, "It's poison."

Her sneer stole the wind from his joyful sails as she looked up, irritated. "What...?" she exclaimed. You imbecile, the amendment was unstated.

"Um... " says the speaker. I'm now feeling incredibly stupid. "That sort of thing. Sodium stearoyl lactylate is a kind of sodium stearoyl lactylate. Monoglycerides. Phosphate of dipotassium." He shrugged his shoulders. Her look on him was unflinching, and she didn't give him a single inch.

"You know..." he finished, his voice trailing off.

"Well, yeah." She appeared unsure whether to be civil or not for a brief moment.

"It's not like it'll make a fuckin' lick of difference, right?" She cocked her head and kept a close eye on his reaction.

He began, "Well, uh... "

Then, all of a sudden, I began to chuckle.

"Actually, no," he said in the end. It felt as if a small but noticeable weight had been removed from his shoulders. "Not even a smidgeon."

She smiled, and they became members of a very special club in that moment because of their shared awareness.

They absolutely understood each other at that point.

She then put the nondairy creamer down, picked up her cup, and returned to her spot in line.

Deitz thought of Jennie as he watched her go away. Would she have been able to comprehend it? He had a feeling she would, but he couldn't be sure; you never knew what was lurking beneath that kind of upbeat air. Under that type of warmth, a lot of uncertainties and unspoken concerns may bloom; a lot of stubborn reluctance to recognize the harsh realities of life...

He reprimanded himself for the second time today, "Waita second." "Remember what you said? Nothing affects you these days.

"You're the happiest man on the planet right now."

It was, of course, correct.

But there were other things that were much easier stated than done.

Chapter Seven

The power of faith, oh, the strength of faith.

Werner Blake adored sitting in the front row of Trinity Lutheran Church. It was an excellent spot for people-watching, and Blake was a social butterfly. He'd sat in this seat every Sunday for the last ten years, watching the sacramental conveyor belt deliver the herd's wine-and-wafer dose.

There was no better place on the planet in his opinion.

Take, for example, this ritual and the concept that fueled it. They named it transubstantiation, though he doubted that more than three individuals in the entire synod could spell the word, much less understand what it meant.

The mystical transformation of wheat and grape wine into not merely symbols of the Eucharist, but the actual flesh and blood itself, was known as transubstantiation. God's kiss breathed eternal life into lifeless glop. It's almost as if it's the ultimate parlor trick.

What did you expect from the world's most successful, longest-running blood cult? There was also something perversely cannibalistic about the whole thing.

What the hell is going on here, As the parishioners filed through, Blake pondered, nodding and smiling. The name of the game is They'll keep coming back for more.

Werner Blake, in his forties and heyday, was a suave, dignified man. He was the director of the Paradise Industrial Development Authority, the lead person for the Paradise Emergency Management Agency, a good citizen, and an all-around community pillar. He was personally responsible for attracting out-of-state industry to the area, resulting in the creation of thousands of jobs and opportunities across the county. He has a lot of contacts. He was a member of the Chamber of Commerce and the Jaycees, lived in Wyndham Hills with his wife and son, and kept a sophomore ski bunny in a condo at Cedar Village. He kept active by playing tennis, flying light planes, and skiing for fun. He ate well, drank responsibly, and slept well at night.

And every Sunday, he put on the wool and went grazing with the flock, clutching his wife's hand and gazing intently into the arched chapel arches. It didn't matter that when he gazed at the massive hung cross, all he saw were sticks, metal, and plaster.

They noticed something. Even if they couldn't see it, they believed it. They came anyway, even if they didn't see it or believe it. That was the game's true beauty. They arrived for the same reasons they thought they should.

Because that's what they're supposed to do.

As the parishioners flowed past, I nodded and smiled...

Werner saw the strength in all that blind faith and obedience. It, like any other natural resource, could be exploited. That's what it was there for, according to Blake. And because Trinity Lutheran was a money congregation, a gold mine for the local Brahmins, seeds planted on Sunday typically bore fruit by the close of business the following Friday.

For him, that was enough of a miracle.

Werner Blake had pushed the boundaries of his decency by the close of services. After all, you could only graze with sheep for so long before your clothing got stifling, your grin a little cramped, and your eyes a little too hard.

Blake nearly welcomed the diversion when Leonard leaned over from the next pew back.

He murmured, "Mornin, Harry." "How are you?"

"Well, uh," Harold began, then paused, his gaze scanning the shadows in the chapel's distant reaches. Blake could now smell the tang of his sweat up close.

"Do you have a problem?" Blake's mind switched to yellow alert in a peaceful manner.

"Yes, I believe so. Yes." Leonard took a deep breath and exhaled forcefully.

"Do you think that can wait?"

There is a little pause.

"Okay." Blake moved in close and tenderly kissed his wife on the cheek. "Excuse us," he said quietly. Carol Blake was lovely, with raven hair and a tight, well-kept appearance.

She was thirty-nine years old and holding. As Blake slid by, she nodded, uninterested. The space next to her that was supposed to be for their son was noticeably empty; Blake glided passed it and into the aisle with a shiny and well-maintained grin.

Blake was then up and moving against the worshipful wave, nodding and smiling as he met the gaze of all those eyes, the many faces of the flock, nodding and smiling and slipping through them with predatory grace.

He didn't turn around to see if Leonard was trailing him. Of course, Leonard was right behind him. What else might Leonards be capable of? You rose or sank on your own merits, based on your inherent value.

Blake was well aware of Leonard's capabilities. Food. But it wasn't quite that straightforward. It would be best to listen to Leonard if there was an issue and he could help.

In a private setting.

"Right now," Blake stated. The chapel erupted in hushed song. Nobody else was in the pastor's office, so it was quiet. "You were saying," I said.

"This morning, I received a phone call." As he spoke, Leonard dry-swallowed. "I got it from a guy I subcontract."

Blake smiled and nodded.

"And, yeah, he said there was an accident or something."

Blake sat in anticipation.

"It was this morning." Blake's eerie silences were terrifying. Leonard accelerated his pace.

"Something has to do with a truck. These people were, uh, disposing of some things with their lads..."

"What kind of chemicals are you talking about?"

"Um... " beats the drums. "Substances that aren't very good." As though it was amusing, Leonard let out a quick hack of laughter. "They were getting rid of some waste—some overstock—when something went awry," says the narrator.

"What kind of garbage...?"

"Werner, my my goodness! I'm not entirely certain! Isn't that all very bad?" Leonard's face flushed, and it occurred to him for a single second that he had just taken his life in his hands and held it up like a bull's-eye on a stick.

Leonard resumed after the Blake made a sympathetic expression.

"As you know, we're in charge of a lot of things." He let out a sigh. Blake encouraged her with a nod. "The majority of it is harmless, but none of it is intended for public consumption.

The point is, these individuals informed me they were properly disposing of it, yet today I got a phone call..."

Blake sat still, his gaze fixed on the scene.

"... claiming that these individuals have been dumping... I'm not sure how I'm going to phrase this..."

"Just say it," says the speaker.

"Christ!" Perspiration beads welled up on his forehead, forming armpit inkblot patterns that met in the middle of his back. "Okay, they were pouring right into Codorus Creek. Straight into the Codorus, which flows into the Susquehanna River, which flows into...who knows where!"

"Slow down." Blake stated it to himself as well as Leonard. He was going through the facts in his head.

"I'm trying to be calm, but this is completely terrifying!" Leonard screamed, hearing himself losing control and attempting to halt it just to see it pass him by. "One of the boys has already died... "

"Ah." The stakes were raised. Blake raised his finger and placed it on his lips, which were pursed.

"... and another youngster is acting strangely; I fear he's been poisoned or something... "

"Okay." Blake brought his finger back and made a reassuring gesture toward Leonard. "Are they the only two people involved?" says the narrator.

Leonard's verbal flow was unexpectedly stifled as he stammered. "I... I believe so. Yes. With the exception of their father. One of their fathers, for example..."

"And who is he?"

"Pusser is his name. He owns and operates a salvage yard just outside of Hellam —"

""What I require is exact information," Blake interjected. Names and addresses are provided. Do you know where the mishap occurred?"

"Have you ever heard of a place named Black Bridge?" "Have you ever heard of a place called Black Bridge?"

"No. However, I'm sure someone has. "What I need from you," he said emphatically, leaning into Leonard as if the fate of the universe depended on it, "are specifics." You know everything there is to know about everything there is to know about everything there is to know In the order you're familiar with."

He took a breath, looked Leonard in the eyes, and double-checked that he'd made eye contact. He'd done so.

"This is something we can handle," he remarked. "There isn't anything we can't handle. We'll be alright as long as we act now and nothing else goes wrong.

Keep that in mind."

Leonard appeared to be relieved. He met Blake's eyes completely for the first time. There was gratitude there, according to Blake.

But, above all, he saw faith.

"Coming to me was the proper thing to do," Blake stated. "Thanks."

"No problem," says the narrator. Leonard was on the verge of blushing.

"Just write everything down for me."

"Right now?"

"There's no better time than now."

Leonard nodded and reached into the pastor's desk drawer, where he discovered a notepad. Blake turned aside as he penned, his mind pondering the options. The worst that may happen is that a scent of this gets into the public air.

On the other hand, there was nothing that couldn't be dealt with in the shadows.

Not a single thing.

"And, Harry?" he inquired, almost casually. "You're not telling anyone about this, right?"

"Certainly not! Oh, my God!" He was informed by Leonard.

Obviously not.

Another religious tenet...

Chapter Eight

The initial shots were high and sharp, like detonating blown-up paper sacks in the distance. Bernard S. Kleigel: the Conscience of a Nation's ears were not deafeningly deafeningly deafeningly deafeningly deafeningly deafeningly deafeningly deafen. As he burnt the goddam backyard leaves, it filtered up from the woods towards him. And it irritated him to no end.

"Billy, you're a jerk! Hold your ground! "He screamed again, his ears straining to hear more. His five-year-old froze in the ready pile, a small Michelin rubber boy, his torso dwarfed by his inflated Osh-Kosh jumper. Billy was no knucklehead. It was lay-low time in the leaf pile after one scent of Dad's voice.

Two additional rounds were fired. Twenty-twos, small-calibre. Bernie's veins in his temples throbbed as he twisted the rake handle so hard that it bent. One word popped into his head—neon, gleaming.

Kids.

Bernie Kleigel was a cardiac time bomb, a coronary car disaster waiting to happen, at the age of 46. He was overweight and overworked, the type of person who got irritated easily and kept grudges that lasted longer than the half-life of plutonium. He lamented his wasted youth, despised the never-ending ravages of middle age, and feared the future.

Millie squeezed the last of the pleasure out of his mid-life crisis when she forced him to participate in one of her wacky fad health regimens. He gave up smoking, as well as alcohol, caffeine, and cholesterol, as well as fried meals and sodium. The quack bastard's doctor was thrilled. Bernie would live another forty years if he kept doing what he was doing, he said. Millie grinned and claimed it was true.

Bernie was a man on the verge of a nervous breakdown.

And here were these youngsters, who had no idea what they had, who had no idea how fragile and precious life was. Didn't they realize such things may blow their little goddam brains out? Maybe it was "accidentally" yours, or someone else's? Christ! When it came down to it, no one was safe in this world full of idiots!

Another shot was fired. Bernie had a distinct mental image of a meat-splattered Rube Goldberg annihilation machine. He noticed the bullet divot in the tree trunk, which was a mile away from its intended squirrelly aim. He observed it pinging off tree after tree, looking aimlessly for something fragile and valuable to damage...

...and then he saw his own little Billy forcefully fly backwards, a scorching red horizontal rain of oil and gristle falling from the top of his skull. He saw himself fall to his knees, deep in the depths of the agony he knew he would experience.

"NOOOOO...!!!" he screamed to himself, as a million depressing worst-case possibilities rustled in his forebrain, itching to play out...

Of course, none of this happened in reality. It's just that it very well may have happened. That was the one thing that no one seemed to get.

That's why Bernard S. Kleigel: the Conscience of a Nation was sorely needed around the world.

"Goddam sonofabitchingkids," he growled, hunkered in his backyard, craning his neck to figure out where they were. By the sound of it, it's somewhere down the hill. I'm heading for the sonofabitching brook.

Although it wasn't technically his property, that didn't stop him from whining about it. His two-acre cleared area of land was bounded by those trees, fercrissake! And it was all documented, every single goddamn inch of it. Trespassing is prohibited. There will be no hunting. I'm not kidding.

Another shot was fired, booming over the forest. Bernie flung down the rake like a gauntlet: the dreaded rake of death. So quickly, he'd have their butts—or their parents' butts—up on charges...

He came to a halt in the middle of his tirade.

And I stood there listening to a flurry of gunshots erupt: a frenetic barrage that shattered the country's silence like a series of cherry bombs. It barely lasted a few manic seconds.

Then it abruptly came to a halt.

Bernie inhaled deeply and felt his heart beat in his Adam's apple. He carefully surveyed the forest line, as if looking for something. The only sound was the wind, which moved through the trees like a burglar through the pockets of a sleeping man.

All of a sudden, it all made sense. He couldn't believe it hadn't happened sooner. He realized these weren't your average hunters, laying down a suppressing fire against the world's birds and bunnies. These were not your typical youngsters.

And there was only one course of action.

He said, "Billy, get in the house." Billy simply stared at him, his eyes blank. "Dammit, there are drug dealers out there! GET UP!"

The Michelin child was energetic, dispersing leaves as quickly as his five-year-old legs would allow. Bernie stormed up the stairs to his small split-level with brick-face siding. A few more of the brick faces had fallen off, revealing the three layers of chicken-wire-reinforced cement, he remarked sourly. He cursed the low-cost siding. I think I'll file a lawsuit against these jerks! The entire goddamn world is collapsing...

Bernie clomped into the entryway and onto the back porch. Millie was making an omelet with Egg Beaters and cottage cheese in the kitchen.

He said, "Goddamned street gangs, here in our backyard!" "I swear to you, I'm not going down without a fight!"

Millie replied on a different frequency, "Of course not, honey." Lite FM 101 is a radio station that broadcasts music. Muzak in one ear and out the other, mental-flossed lovely Muzak: the Rolling Stones' "Paint It Black," as only 1001

Strings could play it. Her fluffy slippers whuffed on the Congoleum as she smiled at him and shuffled across to the breakfast nook. "I hope you're hungry!" says the narrator.

She removed the congealed mass from the pan and placed it on a dish in front of him. He sighed and snatched up the phone, punching three digits with a rage he'd trained.

"There will be hell to pay," he promised. "And the devil doesn't take checks!" says the narrator.

"Of course he doesn't," she assured him, humming along to the melody absently.

County Control was a maze of glass-walled cubicles deep within the Courthouse Building's pale green cinder-blocked guts. County Control was the nerve hub for emergency services, connecting 73 fire departments, 42 ambulance companies, and 55 separate police departments, the majority of which were two-to-five-man borough forces.

Half of Pennsylvania's counties lacked 911 service and would continue to do so for years, putting Paradise ahead of the pack. Despite this, Paradise County was a monument to bureaucratic provincialism: there was no county sheriff, no standardized training, and no guarantee that any of its employees would ever interact with one another, let alone share important job skills.

The complicated web of telephone, computer, and radio communications was managed by an eight-person staff. It was a jumble of cutting-edge and archaic technology, the patchwork survivor of a dozen budget fights. It was on all 365 days of the year, twenty-four hours a day.

It was completely silent at the time.

That was ideal for Dottie Hamm.

She'd just started her shift at eight o'clock, manning the Metro dispatch station with a Spenser book in one hand and a box of Dunkin' Munchkins in the other. A 32-ounce Diet Coke Big Gulp waited by the roadside, waiting to quench the inevitable dry throat.

And Dottie was all set to go.

There were three more civilian police dispatchers on duty, covering the city, county, and rural areas. Jerry and Jean operated the EMS and fire service lines across from the quad. Carol worked near the supervisor's office, conducting warrant searches and APBs. The entire facility hummed with the low nattering of crosstalk, interrupted by beeps and the squelched bark of static, as overstaffed filing cabinets stood beside an IBM mainframe.

All of this was music to Dottie's ears. Sundays were the same way. EMS would almost certainly see some action in the eleventh round. After neighborhood services, there was always some elderly person seizing up with the spirit at the Church of the Nazarene or tripping on the stairs at Zion's Gate and needing to be medevacced to glory. However, most people just hibernated; it was simply too cold to arouse the criminal element.

Days with a warm snap, on the other hand, were a wild card. Anything might happen at any time.

For example, this is one of those days.

Dottie had been working weekends on the second shift for nearly eight years. She was a sweet-faced, potato-shaped woman with a calm demeanor, soothing demeanor, and seemingly endless patience.

Until Bernie Kleigel got in touch with me.

Kelly routed his name, and it appeared on her video monitor seconds later. The monitor was part of an upgraded 911 system that displayed origin information, special stats, and call history for every phone number quickly.

Dottie's molars mashed together when she spotted KLEIGEL.

Under it, some wiseass had typed "10-96." Nutcase was code-slang for 10-96. She was the wiseass. The diagnosis was also validated by the call history list. Kids in the woods every couple of days, like clockwork. There are dogs barking. There will be more children. Trucks making a lot of noise. Children, children, children...

When Dottie closed her eyes, she watched the list go on indefinitely. They'd never seen his face, but they were all too familiar with his horrible nasal voice. It was like lancing a boil with your teeth when Bernie called.

She dusted a fleck of powdered sugar from her blouse before picking up the phone. "Metro dispatch..." she sighed, her fate sealed.

"Dammit, a WAR is going on down here!"

Dottie sighed and rolled her eyes. Dave Dell froze in his swivel chair, crimson face grimacing horrifically, hands locked in a throttling deathgrip around his throat, as he peered up from his desk on the other side of the glass. She immediately recognized the signs and symptoms. He was suffering from a Kleigel attack at the time.

"Now, Mr. Kleigel..." she began, a professional aplomb restraining her giggles. Kleigelitis was a highly contagious disease, therefore she had to be strong.

"Mr. Kleigel, don't 'now' ME!" He barked, his voice a rusty tin razor. "There's some sort of shooting match going on down there. To me, this seems like a drug-related gang conflict! For the love of God, I could've been KILLED!"

Dave enthusiastically endorsed the idea. "Well, that's something we wouldn't want," Dottie remarked.

"Well, you'd best send someone out here before someone gets hurt!"

"I'll dispatch someone straight away."

"You'd better!" says the narrator. Bernie grumbled, his jaw still clenched over the bone. "I'm a tax payer who —"

"Someone will be dispatched straight away. Just take a seat "Bernie's plug was yanked by Dottie.

"You fuckingdickhead," Dave added, slapping Dottie across the face.

"Your mouth!" she exclaimed, but Dottie refrained from cursing. She moaned, "Oh my." "That guy is way too young!"

"You got it!" exclaims the narrator. Dave nodded and tossed his pencil up into the ceiling tile. He flipped his shoulder-length blond hair back and took a more meditative stance, arms behind his head and feet propped up on the low bookshelf where the code manuals were kept. "So, who's going to get the award this time?"

Dottie said, "Bernie's on RD 23." "Hellam Township," as it's known.

Dave joyfully examined the roster sheet to see who was on duty, "Oooh, Adam-sixty." "Hal is his name. Oh, he'll adore this." Dave had a penchant for slapping Hal in the face.

The call card was time-stamped by Dottie. "I'm ninety-six years old. By now, he's most likely out on rounds."

"Of course," says the narrator. Dave smirked and reached across their desks through the sliding glass barrier. He snatched another doughnut hole off the table. "Hal's sprinkled circles are glazed."

"Don't start now." As she pressed the mike send button, Dottie grimaced at her own dwindling snack supplies. "Adam-sixty is the nearest metro station... Do you copy the metro to Adam-sixty? Please come in..."

Dave sat back in his chair, his gaze fixed on his still-attached pencil. His words were hushed. Things would most certainly flare up later: some drunk and disorderly people; possibly a fight. Probably a couple of mishaps.

With any luck, the day would not turn out to be much worse than Bernie the crank's morning diatribe. Dave snatched another doughball from behind the partition. Dottie gave him a gentle slap and continued paging until she was done.

Over the radio, a voice said, "Adam-sixty here." "How's it going, dispatch?"

She began with, "Uh, yeah." "We've received a report of gunshots in the Black Bridge area... "

Chapter Nine

WPAL, the local NBC affiliate, was housed in a two-story brick structure on south Beeker Street in the heart of the city. It was a thirty-person medium-market station with a

150-foot tower on neighboring Mt. Hope to better cover the tri-county broadcast area.

It was a frantic little pressure point on most weekdays.

Weekends, on the other hand, were a different story.

The time was 10:12 a.m. The Studio A control room was deserted at the time. The day shift engineer, John Bizzano, sat slumped in the control chair, half-dozing beneath the amusing papers as he kept everything on the air. On Monitor One, Maria Shriver's Sunday Today was playing quietly. On Monitor Three, CBS Sunday Morning with Charles Kuralt was broadcast. Jerry Falwell, tumescent and arrogant, preened in the center of Monitor Two. Nobody was paying attention to any of them.

The Kirk Bogarde Show was airing downstairs in the editing booth.

Mike Clifford and Laura Jenson packed themselves into folding chairs in front of the console in a room so cramped that they were choking on each other's fumes. Kirk paced behind them, his own televised presence energizing him. He was twenty-five years old and a recent graduate of Brown University, the only son of second-generation wealthy liberal Republicans. Ma and Pa Bogarde had raised their son to be successful, and it was bound to happen.

Kirk put in the effort, to be sure. His Protestant ethics were set in stone, and he was hell-bent on getting his shot. He had methodically crafted the sandy-haired, blandly gorgeous yuppie-drone character that the networks desired, preserving just enough edge to set him separate from the herd, at five-ten, lean, and salon-tanned.

He was dressed in khaki Levi's dockers with red suspenders, a Ralph Lauren button-down shirt with sleeves pulled up to a masculine mid-forearm, and tassel-adorned shoes. He worked out with Nautilus and practiced his deadly instinct three times a week at the Athletic Club's racketball courts.

Kirk knew exactly what he wanted: in ten years, he'd have his own show, giving Geraldo a run for his money.

Laura's objectives, on the other hand, were far less showbiz-oriented. That was most likely why she adored Sundays. The AFC doubleheader was televised on NBC, which meant the six o'clock news was preempted, resulting in no broadcast until eleven o'clock with a skeleton staff on board. As weekend assignment editorcum news director, it gave her plenty of time to catch up: to clean up the shop; to put together the ubiquitous "evergreen" segments, the human-interest and seasonal filler that they always needed and never had enough of; in short, to take care of all manner of unfinished business.

And, of course, there's the eleven o'clock edition to program.

In terms of news, it had been a very quiet weekend. They'd finish up with the network lead as their own, an extra minute of weather to cover last night's storm, and a good eight minutes of sports, complete with the necessary highlights and wrap-ups, if nothing better happened.

And, for God's sake, the obligatory "local narrative."

She shivered. At the moment, that meant keeping an eye on Kirk's proposed follow-up to the contentious "pooper-scooper" legislation that City Council had recently enacted. As his synthesized voice filled the tight booth, she listened.

"...leading to public outcry as neighbors battle the swelling torrent of canine feces," Kirk's TV talking head said. After the bill was passed, anonymous pet activists staged a 'terrorist event,' setting a bag of flaming chairs on the courthouse steps late Saturday afternoon...

"All right," he replied, reaching over Laura's shoulder and lightly stroking her blouse fabric. "Right now is where we cut to the bag," says the narrator.

Mike shifted between the Beta decks in the edit chair. He was the team's youngest cameraman, and he and Kirk were 'PAL's odd couple. He was twenty-two, with a horsey, open face and long stringy blond hair hanging over wire-rimmed aviator-framed glasses. He did bong hits out in his van on slow days. It had been a relatively slow day thus far.

Toggling the knobs, he murmured, "Cutting to B."

The image blipped on the display, switching from Kirk and his microphone to a close-up of a burning paper bag on the courthouse steps. The flames emitted a thick column of black smoke. Laura's face had lost its color.

"Jesus," she exclaimed, stunned. "Do you have any footage?"

Mike smiled as he explained, "Actually, it's a re-creation." "After everyone had left, we shot it."

Kirk grinned. Laura wasn't one of them. The temperature in the psychological chamber decreased by twenty degrees. His narration proceeded.

"...while no one knows what will happen, one thing is certain: the struggle to repeal the pooper-scooper law will continue for some time. WPAL Action News' Kirk Bogarde reports from the county courthouse.

On the screen, a slow-motion close-up of the burning bag emerged, with flames billowing out as a foot came down to trample it. It froze and stayed put.

Mike grinned, mostly to himself, and said, "Awesome." Kirk awaited Laura's response.

"How's everything going?" he asked, grinning. "How do you feel?"

Laura inhaled deeply and exhaled laboriously.

She answered, "Give me a minute to recover."

Laura Jensen, in her mid-thirties, was a tough, cool, and capable lady. She had dark eyes, a thin figure, and an elegant demeanor. She was also smarter than nearly everyone she knew, which developed both her conscience and her cynicism at the same time.

Laura, the eldest daughter of liberal Democratic professionals from New England, had excelled in every class she had ever taken, from kindergarten to the University of Atlanta. Her previous work, with an Atlanta-based CBS affiliate, had ended when her husband's professional relocation took them north to Pennsylvania's backwoods.

Laura had accepted the transition with a sigh of relief, parlaying the culture shock into an upward move in a lateral market. She saw the weekend news director position as a stepping stone up the career ladder, and she wanted to make the most of it.

She was ready for a fight; in fact, she craved it. However, this...

"Words fail me," she replied, fighting the want to rip him to shreds. "First and foremost, I don't think Chris or Tom will appreciate sacks of flaming garbage. Alternatively, our target audience."

"Get real, Jesus." Kirk retorted, refusing to back down. "For chrissakes, City Council was in session for a fucking week overdog turds!" "Besides, it's not even real shit," he continued. We used kerosene to soak some cloths... "

"That isn't the point," Laura snarled. "Kirk, we're a news department! News!" She drew the N-word to emphasize her point. "Okay, this isn't America's Most Wanted. Reenactments are not something we do! Is it possible that I'm getting through to you?"

Laura looked for a glint of understanding in Kirk's eyes. Not even close. One of those days it was going to be. She could already feel the onset of a headache, the kind that would take up residence behind her sinuses and remain all day.

The kind with Kirk's name emblazoned on it.

Weekends were off for Chris Crowley, the genius who'd hired Kirk. Chris was her immediate employer and the news director, reporting to Tom Huntington, the station manager. Laura was in control in the immediate chain of command, putting her butt on the firing line.

She thought it was fantastic. Chris, I appreciate it. Tom, I appreciate it. And, Jesus, thank you.

"All right, tighten it up, and get rid of that goddam bag," she made the decision. "If nothing else comes up, we'll run it."

Kirk had a negative reaction to the biscuit. Laura pressed on, thinking to herself, "Aw." "Do you have anything else?"

On the display, the image blinked out.

Mike exclaimed, "Uh-oh." "It appears to be brunch."

"Oh, sh*t!" exclaims the speaker. Kirk cried as the Beta deck devoured his reenactment in its limitless wisdom. "S**t, s**t, s**t! Is it something you can fix?"

Mike shrugged and pressed the "eject" button. It moaned and slammed shut. To no avail, he jabbed the cartridge with his pen, attempting to shake it loose. Mike shrugged and pressed the "eject" button. It moaned and slammed shut. To no avail, he jabbed the cartridge with his pen, attempting to shake it loose.

He said, "Nope." "I told you, man, by the time they get down here, these decks are smashed." On the heads, there must be fifteen thousand hours. They've prepared themselves for the tar pit."

Laura offered, standing from her seat, "Let's go to Two."

"It's two down," Kirk grumbled.

Mike smiled and nodded. "Maintenance."

"Great," she grumbled, before turning to Mike. "Call Bob and request that he send someone down here right away!"

Mike pushed his way past Kirk and out the door to make the call. Kirk and Laura found themselves uncomfortably near to one another as a result of it. He gripped her shoulder as she rose up and tried to push past him.

He gripped her shoulder as she rose up and tried to push past him. Defiance and denial slam-danced in the airspace between them as their eyes met and held. He pointedly disengaged, his palms up in an ersatz supplication motion.

He pouted as he responded, "So, fine." "It didn't sit well with you."

She said something short and to-the-point. I'm not sure what to say. gesture. "I didn't care for the nonsense... "

"Dog shit," he amended, still moping, though a tiny bad-boy glint slipped into his eye.

That was all it needed, for some reason, to drive her over the edge.

"Listen!" she yelled, and she was bouncing her knuckles off the top of his head before he could react.

"Ow!" His hands were raised. He took a step back, surprised.

"Hello!" she said, rapping her fingers on his head once more. "Mr. Potato Head, hello! Is there anyone at home...?"

"HEY!" He grabbed her hand and held it this time. "DON'T...
"

She growled, "Don't what?"

He came to a complete stop. She had a firm grip on his gaze. He took her hand in his and let go. She hammered home the idea. Throughout it all, they never looked away from each other.

She hissed deep in her voice, "Now you listen to me." "You just shut up and listen if you want to keep your job."

She took a moment to double-check that he had received the message this time. He certainly appeared to do so. His eyes were enormous.

She went on to say, "You're good." "And everyone is aware of it." Your ability isn't the issue here. But if you want to be taken seriously, ditch the infantile nonsense and bring me something genuine... "

"Fine," he snarled, defiantly. "When are you going to tell Medo the truth?"

"When you learn to tell your elbow from your ass." She hoped the words were as icy as she was. "There's a whole world of genuine news to be found! I'll use it if you deliver it to me. Believe me when I say that."

"Why don't you just grow the heck up in the meantime?"

Kirk's focus faltered; for the time being, the eyeball war had been won. She wanted to be happy, but Mudville was still devoid of happiness. He was making the face of an injured puppy.

And, darn her heart, she was feeling guilty once more.

One of 'PAL's worst-kept secrets was their affair: studboy-reporter meets married boss-woman. The movie starts at eleven o'clock. Laura wondered why she'd ever started it more often than she liked to admit; it was yet another piece of unfinished business.

It wasn't simply the age difference, or the IQ point difference, or the fact that he filled some of the gaps left by her previous marriage. In reality, she had no idea what it was. They had no regard for one another. She saw him as a sign of impending calamity for a generation raised on style rather than substance. Both literally and figuratively, he believed she was a tightwad.

It was as if planets collided the first time they fucked.

Every time she said it, she vowed it was the last time.

Laura, on the other hand, stood firm in the station. In a combat, there is no retreat. Ever. She was ready to fire his ass if she had to as his gaze drew back up to meet with hers.

Then the police scanner went off, irrevocably altering their lives.

Officer Hal Thoman had to hump the last stretch of Toad Road on foot after the squad car collided with the first falling tree. He was thinking about Trina the whole time. It left a lot to be desired in terms of substitutes.

Trina was the sultry blonde that worked the night shift at the Mister Krispy donut business. She was just twenty-two years old, and word had it that her personal hygiene routine included shaving in the shade. Hal loathed small-town gossip—small-minded people who knew too much about other people's lives and not enough about their own—but he had to admit he was intrigued in this case.

Their paths had been crossing for a long time as she went off work and he came on, and she'd recently developed a habit of staying much past her shift's end time. Hal appreciated and benefited from this, and had even approached Mister Krispy this morning with the aim of asking her out.

Until the goddamned call came in, of course.

Instead, he was trudging through puddles and muck, chasing down hardened, squirrel-hunting desperados.

Bernard S. Kleigel provided this image.

As he rounded the corner, his cruiser vanished, buried by forests, he thought to himself, "Goddammit, that ain't right." Bernie Kleigel is well-known throughout the county, thanks to his letters to the editors and his goddam nine-one-ones. If ol' Bernie stated there was a drug war in the woods, Hal believed he'd discover Manuel Noriega squaring off against Bigfoot in the century's grudge fight.

If Bernie said there was a drug war in the woods, Hal assumed he'd find Manuel Noriega fighting Bigfoot in a century-old grudge match. He'd left more than his fair share of bullet casings on posted land as a kid. Though Hal couldn't recall any explicit regulation prohibiting individuals from making blazing buttholes of themselves, the more powerful urge was to write Bernie up.

Hal ascended the rutted path, his stylish orange don't-shoot-me vest shining brightly over his outfit. He noted that the storm had ripped the forests to shreds, with downed limbs and broken branches strewn about. He used his trained police eye to list all puddles that were longer than twenty feet or wider than twelve feet. Strangely, the closer he got to the bridge, the less there were.

In fact, he didn't notice any puddles in the short distance ahead. It was as if the ground had absorbed all of the surplus moisture, transforming the road's surface into a near-gelatinous continuum that squashed and yielded a little beneath your feet, taking the imprint of your shoe without ever quite breaking its skin...

Hal jumped when he heard a moist crackle behind him. He spun around and caught the final glimpse of something sliding down the face of an oak tree.It was a magazine-sized slab of bark that left a gooey underpatch in its wake when it dropped.

Hal remarked, "Son of a bitch." Although his vision was great, he began to be concerned by the sights. The exposed stretch of tree skin didn't sit right with me. It prompted him to conduct a brief reality check.

He took a step off the road and immediately noticed that the grass didn't feel right. The blades clung to his soles, but when he ripped them off, they clung to their roots with a scrinching Velcro sound.

For a little moment, I'm lying flat.

Then slowly, methodically pull yourself up.

"This is strange," he thought to himself. He came to a halt, considered it for a moment, and concluded that he was correct. He bent down on his haunches—scrinch, scrunch— and wrapped his thumb and index fingertips around a single blade of grass.

He was bitten by it.

"Yowch!" he exclaimed, clearly astonished. "Goddamn!"

He looked for wounds on his finger, but all he saw was a pinprick of red, veneered by a sticky sheen.

The skin on his hand began to tingle.

Hal took a step back, concerned, and looked over at the oak. He could now see what was wrong with this image.

He could now see the unsettling, microscopic array of undulating grub-things digging blindly into the punky, fibrous interior...

He flashed back, "I've been in these woods a thousand times, but I've never seen anything like this." It was as if a plague had struck, wreaking havoc on the trees and the planet itself.

He saw the bridge through the woods.

And for the first time, I became aware of the vehicle.

Hal Thoman was filled with dread and a foul aching in the pit of his stomach. From this vantage point, the truck appeared to be completely messed up. If there was a pattern here, it wasn't a particularly nice one.

He murmured, "Son of a bitch." "I'm Adam-sixty, and I'm calling from County. Do you plagiarize?" He talked into his phone. The signal was bounced back to the cruiser, which then boosted it back to County Control.

The dispatcher's voice, salted with dropouts and static, came back over the box on his hip, "Roger, Adam-sixty." "How much is your twenty?"

"Roger, County," he said, "I'm out at Black Bridge." "I've got an abandoned truck parked on the roof." It appears that the ten-seven vehicle reported this morning is the culprit. He went on to say, "Whoever took it left it pretty blasted." "I'm taking a look at it."

Roger, Take care when approaching."

He answered, "You got that correct." "Adam-sixty out,"

As he walked out onto the bridge, Hal recognized that caution was not the word. It didn't exactly convey the emotion. Dread was a better word. He nervously laughed, "Oughta be a new code." Approach with trepidation.

The creek's roar engulfed him, filling his mind with thunder. The rails and gravel bed were greasy and sticky with waste oil under his feet. Tar. Worse is yet to come. The sensation had crept up his arm and lodged like a big knot of strain in his shoulder.

All of that, though, was dwarfed by the sight of the truck.

He believed "blasted" was an understatement. They simply nuked the jerk. It appeared as if a huge insane toddler had driven his Tonka truck straight to hell. The driver's door was hung open, mangled, and the glass were gone. Safety glass chunks surrounded the frames like broken teeth stubs. In a thousand spots, the paint job was damaged and ashen, flaking down to the metal.

On and around the truck, there were around a dozen barrels. He realized he hadn't been burned. Blistered. Like the truck, for example. The caps had blown off. A white sludge residue oozed from one, oozing into the stony track bed.

Hal walked carefully through the minefield, taking care not to step on anything. He approached the passenger side and read the inscription that was still visible on the door. "Aha," he exclaimed as he peered into the taxi.

The ignition keys were still in the car.

He said, "Bingo." "You sons of bitches, I got you." Keys were rarely used by thieves. Trina's personal habits weren't the only topic of conversation on the gossip circuit. The Pussers got their fair portion, too, and none of it was good, unlike Trina's.

Now and then, lowlife hunks of dung had guardian angels who would protect them. And sometimes, if you wanted to get along in the world, you had to turn your back. He'd had to swallow that bitter pill at least a thousand times as a cop.

However, if you wanted to defy the odds and try your hand at true justice, you required proof. As in the case of physical proof.

This one didn't require a rocket scientist to put together. He thought he was going to explode just seeing all those empty barrels and the truck pulling up with its tailgate dangling over the side.

He screamed, "I ain't sure what happened here," but "I'm about to find out." And when I do, you're going to be nailed to the fuckin' walls. It's true.

He read the plates off the front and replied, "Adam-sixty to County." "Thomas X-Ray three nine nine three is the Pee-Aye license number. We may have a Hazardous Materials (HazMat) issue here..."

He returned his gaze to the toasted barrels, pausing to weigh his remarks. "Perhaps we should switch to Echo-Four, County," he suggested, only now considering the ears that might be listening in. In the handset, there was a sharp bark of static. "Uh, County?" says the narrator.

His lips were quivering with pleasure.

"Jesus!" Kirk blurted, his thoughts racing. "Did he say exactly what I believe he said?"

Laura said, pushing back the scanner's volume and grabbed a pencil, "God, let's hope so." When the call initially came in, it exploded through the news department like a bomb blast because she'd cranked up the controls while they were in editing.

Laura looked at a map and doodled. This was a godsend: a stolen truck could only hold a thirty-second fill—or a whole sixty if it was completely wrecked. But this... this had potential. This could spare her from the wrath of the pooper-scooper.

Kirk, on the other hand, was practically gagging. The split had muddled the signal, but not before he'd heard that magical word. It was his big break, the ticket to the stars he'd been waiting for.

HAZMAT. Hazardous Substances. The moonmen, to be precise.

My God, he exclaimed. If there has been an accident...

"I'm on it," he said as he walked up the stairwell. Mike emerged in the camera bay doorway in the backdrop, mounted up and ready to roll.

"Wait, wait!" says the narrator. Laura, notepad in hand, called after him. Her hair fell across her face as she listened to the scanner transmission on tape with one ear, nodding rhythmically and scribbling.

"Wait? What are you waiting for?" Kirk shifted his weight as he walked out the door.

Laura ripped the sheet of paper from the pad and said, "For this." "It's a lot easier if you know where you're going."

Kirk returned to her with an embarrassed nod. "Thanks."

Laura leaned across the desk, her body formal but her eyes bright. It's possible that this will be a hot topic. Don't mess with it.

Kirk took the paper, and their fingers came together. The spark has resurfaced. It'll be damned to hell by God.

"Get in the car," she said. "And make sure you're in radio contact." He bolted up the stairs, nodding yes, yes, yes,

"KIRK!" she said as he rounded the corner. He came to a halt and returned his gaze to the newsroom.

"Okay, just the facts. Please bring me something genuine."

Kirk winked and smiled.

After that, he vanished.

Inside his skull, it was buzzing.

"No no no," Hal screamed at himself, as if his consciousness was a bargaining chip. He acted as if he could urge the molecules in his brain to leave. The buzz in his inner ear was a high faraway whine that scared the living daylights out of him. He had no idea what it was. He had no idea what it did.

He did, however, have a strong understanding of where it came from.

A voice in his head screamed, "Get away from the truck!" This is sound advice. Hal grabbed it, took three steps, then collapsed, falling forward and tripping over a railroad tie. He was hurled toward the cliff at the bridge's edge by his momentum.

He just managed to catch himself, his stomach painfully lurching as it slammed into the ledge. Semidigested Mister Krispy Kreamy Kake sluiced from his nostrils and throat.

He exclaimed, "Oh, gosh."

And he looked down over the edge.

The creek was churning, black and deep, bloated with rain and incredible strength as it burst its banks, rushing swelled and insanely angry toward the river beyond.

It was like looking down into the eye of a hurricane at the churning ground below.

The brittle bees that lined the shore had been pummeled by the storm, violated and depleted; what blanches remained were joined together and rustled like wounded leper limbs. Broken branches and uprooted trees, old tires, rusted machine parts, bottles and cans, and runoff detritus, all caught at loggerheads and hammered by the water, blocked up sections of the creek.

The pain in his eyes was like napalm, and it clouded the lenses of his eyesight. The murky greens and browns of the woods became more intense, as if someone had turned up the color saturation on a poor old TV set to the point where the entire landscape pulsated with garish, oversaturated hues.

In a tangle of flotsam near the overflown bank, Hal noticed a glimmer of light twitching and sparkling above the water's surface. It flickered again, and he caught on to it, pulling it as sharply as he could into focus. It was flat, polished, and disk-shaped.

A gleaming tiny disk

On a delicate, slender wrist...

"Oh, fuck!" exclaims the speaker. Officer Hal Thoman groaned, his stomach churning up more excrement. Bernie Kleigel and his pint-sized war fatalities had entirely escaped his mind.

They were, however, as large as death.

After all, it was the Hinds lads.

Ralph and Jimmy J., eight and ten years old, were half-submerged, knotted together as though wadded and flung there, and impaled a dozen times on the errant ends of the spreading debris pontoon.

They had their eyes open. They were talking with their lips open.

In the holes, wet things crept around.

He stumbled away, gasping, after saying, "Oh, Lord." One of their arms, pale as a china ghost, jutted out of the water, hooked in timber, muck, and mire. Jimmy J.'s Timex was the gleaming object that had drew his attention.

It was attached to the hand that was pointed palm up, fingers curled carefully around the empty area. It bobbed in the strong stream, as if beckoning him to come down.

His intellect warned him to get off the bridge. Remove yourself from the goddamned bridge.

Hal swung around, clamping down on the adrenaline rush before it turned into full-fledged terror. He dashed away from the structure as quickly as his legs could take him. With each passing yard, his brain cleared a bit more, until he was safe.

I was standing on the wrong side of the bridge.

Oh, that was clever, he thought. So, what's next? Between him and the rest of the world was the bridge. The bridge belonged to the vehicle. He remembered the phone and grabbed it. "Adam, sixty miles to the county..."

He twitched as a sharp bark of static clipped into his ear, causing an involuntary spasm. "County, come in..."

Nothing.

He screamed, "Goddamn it!" as he slammed the box against the cliff. Dead spots were widespread in the hinterlands: undetectable pockets of interference, confluences of topography obscuring transmission. It happened on a regular basis. However, it was still as if your connection had been severed, leaving you alone and exposed...

"I'm in desperate need of some BACKUP!"

The radio hissed and spit out lifeless air.

"NOW, GODDMAMTT!" .

Something shattered beneath him.

He was surprised and exclaimed, "Wah!" As if shocked from a dream, his right hand awoke on the butt of his revolver.

The dam was beginning to crumble beneath the surface of the river. "Fuck!" As he descended the rough slope toward the creek, Hal exclaimed. The water was driving the swaying mass against the bridge, causing the debris to break apart. As it flooded through, the river gathered up speed, sucking up flotsam like stew through a straw.

Oh, jesus, he exclaimed. If they get through, we'll have to drag them back across the river. The thought made him nauseous, making him sicker than the poisonous gases. He was well acquainted with their parents. In his mind's eye, he could see their distressed expressions: a piercing, near-precognitive flash of terror.

And he was desperate to get out of here, to get the fuck going so he wouldn't have to look back. However, their bodies were close enough for a snag to occur. He was confident in his assertion.

He didn't have a choice because of the situation.

As he skittered down the moss-crusted boulders that slanted into the creek, he murmured, "This sucks." "This is terrible."

Hal reached the water's edge and stood in the shadow of Black Bridge, peering at the creek's and pylon's intersection. The bank was swollen and slick, and the water was stygian and decaying. Hal steadied himself by picking up a long, thick branch.

As he stepped into the room for the first time.

Cold flooded his shoe, gluing his sock and pants leg to his shin. He mumbled through clinched teeth, "Oh man, this really,really sucks," his particular mantra of misery and fear.

He took another cautious step forward, his other foot engulfed by the frigid blackness, and measured the distance between the bodies. He estimated a maximum distance of twenty feet.

He reasoned that it might as well be twenty miles. Alternatively, 20,000.

He took another stride forward.

His leg had sunk to the middle of his thigh.

He screamed, "Whoa—SHIT!" as he desperately stabbed the branch into the water for assistance. His left foot pushed up and found traction on a hard 45-degree angle. Like a drunk walking a white line, he weaved back and forth.

He said, "Bad idea." "That was a bad fucking idea..."

Something moved in the water: a current inside a current, a dense sinew of liquid pushing against the stream's pull. It swept by him like an eel, then quickly turned around.

And it sank heavily between his legs.

The first wave of panic hit hard: a tidal wave crashing down, obliterating the serenity. He whinnied in his throat and considered his options: sphincter irising shut and applying for a promotion, or a heart wrecking-ball slamming a hole in his chest.

He thought to himself, "Fuck this." Drag the river like a goddamn goddamn goddamn goddamn god I'm leaving right now.

Hal walked away.

He couldn't do it.

He moaned, "Shit!" His right foot was caught in the muck up to his ankle.

Silt sucked at his sneaker with a voracious appetite. Twigs and filthy chunks of mud clung to his legs like pier pilings' froth. He screamed and searched around blindly with his left foot, leaning hard on the branch.

It landed on something spherical and flat. With just one taut inch of sheet-metal give, it seemed sturdy. As if it were the hood of an automobile.

Alternatively, the apex of a barrel...

Oh, God, he thought, and a wave of terror washed over him. Oh, my goodness. The truck on the bridge comes to mind. He twisted and turned his right ankle fiercely trying to release himself, then yelled as he pressed his left foot against the drum head and pushed with everything he had...

...and his right ankle popped like a firework as his left foot ripped through the barrel's deteriorated skin: sharp metal rim cutting his flesh from calf to buttocks, encasing his entire left leg in steel and frigid corrosive agony. He sank on his stomach, his pistol belt sunk with him. The radio shorted out and ignited.

Hal shrieked, turned into an uncomfortable side-stance, his left leg sticking out at a pelvis-cracking angle, and clutched the branch hard enough to peel bark. His shoulders drooped and sunk into the water. He battled to keep his head above water, winning by a razor-thin margin but losing his hat in the process. It landed brim-high in the water and sped off and into the flume like a small boat.

It was a farcical comedy, but no one was laughing. Hal's face was inches above the surface now, his body carried down by the current and his so-called water-repellent jacket, which had turned into a leaden sponge, voiding all manufacturer's warranties. His right ankle was throbbing uncontrollably. His left leg ached like it had been soaked in a lye-and-acid stew.

He yowled, "HELP!"

His pleas were drowned out by the sound of the dam before they ever left his mouth. Water was pounding at an alarming rate through the center arch, and the entire mass was rapidly sucking in on itself like a great damp black hole. Jimmy J. slipped beneath the water's surface, his Timex still ticking, his body dragged into the slipstream and carried away.

To Hal's side, debris floated freely around him, forming a line for the slide. Little Ralph's arm reemerged from the water only ten feet distant, appearing increasingly like a wax mannequin left in a window display for too long.

The arm slid a little lower and drew a little closer.

The fingers began to move.

Hal let out a deafening squeak of disbelief. The hand sank once more. The jagged metal collar slashed the damp flesh of his inner thigh like a ripsaw as he turned toward the bank.

Hal noticed the water becoming dark almost instantaneously and felt the scorching spritz of seeping fluid that was feeding it. The scream followed the pain a few moments later.

The dark cloud became larger.

The little hand, wet and red, came up in the middle of it, way too close.

"Oh, for the love of God, please!" He stutters and burbles. As he struggled forward, a thick plume of water burst up beneath the surface, like an underwater fountain.

He compared it to peeing in the tub. Oh, my God...

As he joined with the flow, the river pounded, squeezed, and drained him, eating his life. Tiny fish-things nibbled at the exposed skin beneath the surface, nursing his open wounds and inhaling his blood.

The body of the dead boy was not far away. Cold, swollen tiny limbs moved in the slipstream, catching against him. From the shadows emerged a face, its eyes half-open and milky, its tongue coyly protruding.

Hal screamed and struggled, his spray-blind and dwindling eyes fixed on the heavens.

That's when he noticed the stranger, who was looking down from the bridge above.

He had a crazed thought: Bazooka Joe.

He has the appearance of Bazooka Joe.

The figure stood against the ominous sky, blackly silhouetted. His leather jacket was mud-caked and clotted, much like the moss-like mass of black hair that hung like moss across his brow, blocking his vision.

His jaw was covered by a filthy red kerchief.

Ralph's clammy fingers fluttered across his forehead, tracing awkwardly down his features as Hal strained to yell for help. As the fingertips groped past his eyelashes, he squeezed his eyes shut in terror, hanging just a fraction of a second too long before dragging down to clamp on his bottom lip.

But the current was too powerful, the flesh too thin, and he let out the last scream of his life as his lip tore loose, spritzing, and peeled down to his chin.

I'm staring up at the man on the bridge, helpless.

After all, who'd opted to assist him?

He'd snatched a barrel from the rails and lifted it high above his head. As if he were throwing a rope, he let fly with it suddenly, aiming directly for Hal's face.

It seemed like it took an eternity to get there. End over halt, growing larger and larger, a spinning black speck that encompassed Hal's vision in a split second before bursting in brainpan shrapnel, bringing the light to a wet crashing end.

He left the top of his head open.

For the new mind, the Overmind, to settle down.

It was only a matter of seconds before the dam completely burst.

And the next world burst out, living and unconstrained.

Chapter Ten

There was a problem with the reactor.

Fred Jenkel scratched his head and examined the meter, which was one of several that monitored nearly every element of the plant's operations. Even though Jenkel was confident Westinghouse was working on it, it appeared like the only moving elements of the plant that didn't have a needle hooked to them were the human ones.

The city is twenty-two miles southeast of the city, on the rocky banks of the Susquehanna River in Delta Township.

During the post-TMI/Chernobyl industry slump, the Wolf's Head Nuclear Generating Station was one of the few plants to be completed. It had been running smoothly for four years, meeting the ever-increasing demand for power in the greater Valley metro area.

Jenkel slumped back in his chair, his bald place absently fingered. He was a huge man with a big beaky nose and the jowly, cheerful face of a favorite uncle, and he'd just returned from a vacation-fishing trip in the Poconos. He'd caught three fish and had a bad case of sunburn, and his browned pate stood out like the bulb of an overheated thermometer against the white of his shirt. He cocked his head, his brow furrowed in thought.

He'd almost accidentally discovered the flux in the neutron population twenty minutes before. It was a minor rise in temperature and power, well within the reactor coolant's normal plus-or-minus boundaries. He'd caught it during a routine spot check, dutifully recorded the reading, and then proceeded to level it by releasing a stream of borated water into the core's closed-loop system.

The boron performed its molecular function, slowing the reactor by regulating the fission process. Jenkel had executed the procedure countless times before in his role as the nuclear half of the day shift's Reactor Operator Team. Borate the coolant and keep an eye on the temperature while the power goes off. It was as though the fission process had been fine-tuned, and it always functioned perfectly.

However, the temperature had risen once more. Odd.

Jenkel went to his younger, less experienced other half, whose duties in charge of the turbines and steam generators at the time consisted of snickering at every other paragraph of Dave Barry's column in the Sunday News. According to the training, once a pressurized water reactor was up and running, they could practically go home and leave the reactor to operate itself. Normally, it was completely accurate. It was, however, a homily with its own disclaimer, a caveat akin to a void if removedtag.

Unless something unexpected happens...

"Hah!" Bob Henkel let out a piercing bark that rang out in the otherwise silent control room. "This guy cracks me up," says the narrator. He burst out laughing. "Isn't he suggesting that we convert the federal deficit to voltage?" Then pass it through electrodes linked to each member of Congress's genitals... "

"Hey, Bob," Jenkel interjected, interrupting the conversation. "Take a look at this."

Henkel raised his head, his blue eyes glistening with delight. He was twenty-nine years old, svelte as a beanpole, and the physical polar opposite of Jenkel. With the exception of the snout, which was large and slanted downward, it was so similar to Jenkel's that they may have come from the same Play-Doh Monster Schnozz kit. When you combine that with their names, the jokes were bound to happen.

Henkel rose from his seat and strolled over. "How's it going, boss?" he inquired.

Jenkel replied, "For one thing, the reactor load." "Take a look at the core." With his chin, he motioned to the meter.

"The neutron count has skyrocketed." Henkel shrugged as he examined the scenario. He offered, "So borate the water."

Jenkel said, "I already did." "Now it's up and running again."

Henkel pondered the situation, as well as the older man's interested rather than anxious tone of speech. He, like

Jenkel, was well aware that they were continually building up and letting down water for the core vessel, filtering out particulates or ions before re-entering the loop. Henkel pondered aloud if this was some sort of test, an impromptu spot-quiz by ol' Dead Fred to jolt the shift along.

"Should I add NutraSweet?" he wondered.

Jenkel fixed his gaze on him, but he was not smiling. After all, this could have been serious. Jenkel said, "Go get Sykes." "Inform him that we may have a problem."

The younger man's smile vanished as his eyes leveled with Henkel's. Bob swung around and dashed over to the open door of the superintendent's office. He began, "Uh, Mr. Sykes..."

Fred Jenkel, on the other hand, was no longer paying attention. His ears were tuned to another sound, a subsonic drone that he felt rather than heard, emanating from a nearby humming structure. It could have been on the moon from his radiation-shielded, hermetically sealed vantage point.

The meter's needle rose then leveled off, only to scoot up again a few moments later. Flutter... flutter... flutter... flutter... flutter...

He persuaded himself, "It's nothing," dismissing memory, intuition, and experience. "Nothing at all," says the narrator.

Jenkel kept an eye on the situation. While doing so, I kept thinking to myself, "The reactor could nearly operate itself."

Ascend...

Unless, of course, anything went wrong...

Chapter Eleven

Gwen Taylor adored the act of creation above all else.

She was clad in sweatpants and a paint-splattered blouse stolen from Gary as she stood in front of her nearly finished work-in-progress. On the hefty glass sheet that served as her palette, blue and yellow were combined with a touch of white. Three hues merged to form teal as they swirled together.

She dipped her brush in water, picked up some paint, and held it in the air. "All right, your Highness," she murmured as she examined her prey. "Greatness is on its way."

Gwen drew her weapon and fired.

The Faery Queen's left cheek came to life on the nursery wall. The right was quickly ornamented with a double slash. Gwen worked quickly and clumsily, displaying incredible talent and dexterity in the most inexplicable of movements. She dabbed here, brushed there, and in no time, a coating of cool green had blossomed across the mural's width.

"Yes... yes... The speakers of her spattered studio boom box jingled with David Byrne's "Rei Momo." Gwen took a brushful of magenta and splattered it on the shadows around the figure. She winked and said, "This is a good look for you."

The nursery was breathtaking, a beautiful combination of innocence and mystery. Stuffed animals dangled from a hammock in the corner, ready for little hands to bring them to life; an antique oak crib, meticulously refurbished by Gary, took up one entire corner of the room, a tempo rarity hidden beneath a protective drop cloth. Above it, a mobile floated slowly, swaying in an almost imperceptible breeze. It was a room filled with unfulfilled dreams.

Gwen couldn't wait to show it to Spike.

She set the brush down and picked up a finer one to add some yellow highlights. She then took a raggedy sponge she'd custom-plucked for maximum texture and began patting the fresh paint's surface, creating a stippled coral look.

It was a method that her art school painting instructors would have scorned, but screw 'em. Gwen was a big believer in proper technology misuse.

After all, need isn't the genuine mother of invention, she reasoned.

Weirdness is what it is.

Gwen was a one-of-a-kind individual. Her teachers despised her manner, which was eccentric and unschooled but full of fire, attractive in its imagination and sheer zeal. They told Gwen Kessler, a young artist, that she'd make an excellent hairdresser. One informed her he now saw why past generations liked their women to be barefoot, pregnant, and in the kitchen; another even proposed in front of the entire class that she should enroll in the matchbook painting school. Make Big $.

So when she got tired of being spit on by the Atlanta College of Modern Art's hierarchical cliques of snooty conceptual types, she quit. She retaliated by declaring herself a postmodern neoprimitive guerilla cartoonist and holding her own one-woman protest display outside the school's main door, which also served as the Peachtree Road entry to the prominent and staid Atlanta Museum of Modern Art. She sprayed the title of her point on the wall. It was smarmy and titillating, and it was entirely aimed for yocks, and it completely missed the mark.

The videographer acquired her phone number off the rap sheet, thought about her for a day, and then contacted her. He expressed regret. She refused to accept. He asked her out on a date.

She kindly told him to go fuck himself.

He then went on to look up the date of her arraignment. He was waiting for her when she arrived. By that time, she'd established herself as a little celebrity, although an embarrassment: Channel Two followed up on her case on a regular basis, usually airing the same smarmy tape of her thrashing, bare-butted arrest.

He asked her out once again. She recognized him from the television crew and requested that he respect her privacy.

He was back at her court appearance. She was sentenced to six months of probation. He presented her with a rose and a gift in a brown paper bag. On the way home, she cracked it open in the cab.

A note with his phone number was included in the envelope. Everyone deserves a second opportunity, according to the note.

She took the present out of the package and opened it. A couple of three-quarter-inch videotapes were found inside. There are two types of masters: masters and dubs. It's all there.

That night, and for the rest of the year, Channel Two did not broadcast any coverage.

The next day, Gwen called the cameraman to express her gratitude. He apologized again and said it was his pleasure, but he didn't even ask her out.

She called him again three days later. He invited him to lunch this time, which was a special treat for her. Yes, he said. Everyone is entitled to a second opportunity.

Gary Taylor was the cameraman's name.

And, as they say, the rest is history...

The memory made Gwen blush. It had been a long journey from Atlanta to here, and she couldn't believe she was the same person. Gary and she had traveled extensively, from Atlanta to Chicago to New York, always following Gary's performances. She preferred some areas to others, but they were all fertile ground for learning and growth.

None of them, though, seemed like home.

It was a straightforward, if all-consuming, requirement. From the pages of magazines, from the gushings of friends who lived upstate, and from a clear smell of breeze in the stuffy summer air of their too-small Chelsea flat, home began to appeal to them.

After a while, they both realized that New York was too expensive, too polluted, and too crowded to grow old or have children in. Gary didn't have an actual hometown, so it ruled out a lot of possibilities.

Exodus.

Overall, she'd been happier: less irritable, less anxious. The house was fantastic, and she had a lot of fun renovating it. She went on hikes and to the farmer's market, and she lived a much nicer and softer life. Her world seemed to be coming together with the arrival of the Spikester. What more could a person ask for?

Even yet, it chafed on occasion. She felt strangely normal in this place. She didn't have faith in it. Yes, it was clean here, with a far lower crime rate and a cost of living that was half that of the rest of the country... a true "quality of life" place, according to LifeStyle magazine. However, there was no art scene to speak of, a lackluster nightlife, and just a small number of restaurants worth visiting. She was divided between the wildass and the earth mother, the hellion and the homebody Gwens inside her.

And now there's a third on top of it. Gwen/not Gwen is nesting in her stomach. The one who was so much a part of her and Gary's relationship, but was ultimately different. The one who was greater than the sum of its components.

The one who would address her as "mother."

She was unsure if it was a good thing, just as she was unsure about routine, responsibility, and all the other trappings of adulthood. She was concerned that the day-to-day grind would sap her imagination and gradually rob her of her oddness. Leave her shut off from the Mystery's essence.

She knew better on the inside. Her inner voice confirmed her suspicions. It was stated that mystery is more than a fashion or a way of life; mystery is a state of mind.

Gwen wished to believe in herself. She'd always done so. But she'd been thinking lately; there was something about returning here that blew through her like a nasty wind now and then. Saying that staying here is the kiss of death, that it will suffocate you, that it will rob you of your sense of the mysterious...

Gwen shook her head. She told herself, "Stop it." "You're making a fool of yourself."

The Faery Queen smiled knowingly on the wall, becoming more real with each stroke. Gwen had completed ninety-nine percent of the painting and was determined to complete the hundredth stroke before Micki arrived in town. Spike, for example.

Whichever came first was the winner.

Gwen actually cared about her work, which was unusual by any definition. She'd persevered over the years, parlaying her strange vision into a relatively successful art career, doing fantasy and science fiction, as well as the occasional horror paperback, but most notably covers for Micki Bridges'Bob-Ramtha! series. Micki's contracts always included a clause requiring Gwen Taylor covers, and her publishers were happy to oblige with over eight million copies in print. As a result, a lifelong friendship gained the added benefit of professional fulfillment.

Plus, as Micki frequently reminded her, we got to write about our lunches together. Gwen smiled as she worked mottled black and neon green streaks into the cape's fabric.

The Faery Queen was one of the archetypal figures portrayed in Micki's writings, and Gwen had elected to hang her on the nursery wall for that reason. Gary and Gwen had promised long ago that there would be no Smurfs for the Spikester. They desired for their child to grow up in the embrace of the Mysterious.

The Faery Queen was a royal entity who personified the Spirit of the Living Earth. She was part animal, part insect, part fish, and part fowl. Her hair was a cascade of feathery plumage, and her garments were a luxuriant drapery of green living plants. Her features were arthropodal in nature, exquisitely humanoid but with a chitinous exoskeleton. Her thorax swelled into fully human breasts, and her body was wasp-waisted and segmented. Her fingers were long and delicate, and her feet were delicately cloven, doe's feet.

She held a white candle in her left hand. A little star shone in her right hand. Her throat and neck were covered in a rainbow of smooth scales, and a lovely amulet glistened on a fine golden chain.

She was angry, domineering, and even cruel in earlier images; however, Gwen softened the effect by giving her a wise smile and warm blue eyes, as well as surrounding her with birds, rabbits, and other delicate creatures, transforming her into a benign sort of otherworldlyÜbermother.

However, Gwen added cheekbones as an afterthought. Beautiful cheekbones.

Gwen took a step back to assess her work, her brow furrowed in concern. This was the most important project she'd worked on during her pregnancy. She wished for perfection.

"Something's off," she said, and the answer was obvious the moment she uttered it. "A-HA!"

She put a fine brush in the paint and gently painted a dot of white to the blue of the Faery Queen's eyes.

Adding a glimmer of vitality.

"That's it," Gwen remarked, content for the time being. She looked at her wristwatch. "How's that for timing?" she exclaimed to her coworker. "It's time for us to begin moving."

She gathered her brushes and walked over to the sink.

The Faery Queen stood on the wall, watching her walk away.

Gary, on the other hand, knelt in the garage, honing his own gentle art of motorbike repair.

His scoot was a bespoke Harley-Davidson softtail from the year 1988, and it was his pride and joy. In the winter of 1989, he tore it down and rebuilt it with a ninety-six-inch S&S stroker kit, completely altering it. Gary had a natural instinct for tools and technology. Gary Taylor could figure out what made things tick, whether it was mechanical, electrical, or digital.

He worked for WPAL as a bench engineer. He was primarily responsible for equipment repairs, transformer maintenance, and a monthly review of the broadcast tower and microwave uplink, but he was well-qualified to handle any broadcast crisis.

As far as gigs go, it was a good one. However, it was still only a job.

Gary worked to live, not the other way around.

He'd been up on farms as the son of migrant workers, which was a fancy way of saying he'd grown up rough. There was a lot of drifting, a lot of backbreaking, tedious scrabbling in the dirt, and not much in return. On more than one occasion, he'd had to assist in the birth of cattle while also drowning a litter of kittens on the same day. He'd experienced true hunger, not the what's for supper, nothamburger again sort, but the bottomless dull-knife gnawing in your stomach that's the last thing you feel at night and the first thing you feel in the morning. He'd experienced adversity, hopelessness, and despair, and he'd pulled himself out of it all by his own bootstraps.

At the very least, the event had given him a new viewpoint. When life throws you a curve ball, turn it into fertilizer. He'd be just as happy raising mutant cows with Gwen if the nukes hit tomorrow and they survived.

Gary nudged the catch pan under the engine block with his leg as he reached under the block and loosened the crankcase bolt. The softtail appeared stock on the exterior, but he'd tuned and cranked it till it was two hundred and forty hp of flat-out drag bike, barely street legal. Gary had never actually cranked it above one-twenty, and not much over ninety since Gwen put the bun in the oven, but it could go a buck and a half without breaking a sweat.

Oh well..., he reasoned. I guess I'm becoming more conservative as I get older.

On the radio, Little Feat was playing. Allow it to flow. Bright streamers of light flowed in via the open garage door. Gary was looking forward to one last ride before the cold set in: ripping down some back roads, going nowhere, and loving every minute of it.

Gwen appeared behind him, a steaming mug already in her hands, and said, "Hey, Dad." "Would you like some coffee?"

"Thank you, Mom," I say. Gary rose to his feet and turned toward her, kissing her and accepting the Java.

"Ick, you're all slimy," she remarked as she backed away.

He nuzzled her and murmured, "Thought you loved slimy."

"Not like that," she murmured as she pushed by him and walked over to the door. "You'd better get yourself cleaned up, babe. By eleven o'clock, we must be at the airport..."

"Blech!" Gary jumped right in. He frowned and glanced at his cup with a bitter expression. "What's up with this coffee?" says the narrator.

Gwen seemed surprised as she said, "I just cooked it." "What's the matter?"

"It's disgusting to eat. That is all there is to it." Gwen took the cup from him and sniffed it. There was an obnoxious, acrid stench.

Gwen shrugged, her face flushed. "I'm not sure; I acquired it from a small shop in the Galleria. It's already quite costly."

Gary replied, "Yeah, well." "They received it from the incorrect Valdez," says the narrator. He cynically hoisted the steaming mug. "Exxon coffee is the richest type of coffee."

She didn't make a sound. He took another sniff of the coffee. He recoiled and murmured, "Yech." The milk had curdled into a mottled curlicue shape that spun gently in the center of the cup, resembling a question mark. "Fuck it," he grumbled as he poured the rest into the waste-oil pan. Then he handed Gwen the empty cup. "Thanks anyway, darling," says the narrator.

She accepted it with a shrug. "Next time, make it yourself."

He responded, "Shit, babe, I didn't mean anything by it," but she had already walked away.

She called over her shoulder, "Better get ready," and slammed the door shut a little too hard.

Gary shivered. He sobbed, "I'M SOR-REEE...!"

In answer, the thud of cupboard doors banged shut. "Shit," Gary moaned as he washed off with a glob of GoJo from the can at the utility sink. "You're not going to win."

Pregnant women get up to the strangest things, he lamented. Hormones, For christ's sake, she's in the slammer for disrespecting her stupid special-occasion fifteen-dollar-a-pound yuppiecoffee. I can't wait for this to be over.

Meanwhile, all he could do was practice his eggshell softshoe and hope that nothing else went wrong.

The phone began to ring.

"Oh no," he exclaimed, his gaze falling on the cordless Cobra on the workbench. The phone didn't ring this early on a Sunday for one reason: it wasn't to wish him a pleasant day off. He washed his hands, wiped them on his jeans, and finger-combed his hair while waiting for the caller to hang up.

It was pointless. The fourth ring was the one he picked up on.

He sighed, "What is it, Bob..."

"How did you figure out it was me?" Bob Dobberman inquired, clearly perplexed.

Gary said, "Experience." "Bob, let's go right to the point."

Bob "The Knob" is a character in the film "The Knob." Gary's boss, Dobberman, was a rotund and jovial technogeek who wore a pocket protector and had a basement full of ham radios. He was the head engineer at 'PAL, and he lived for his job: Sigma Delta Theta, Society of Broadcast Engineers, all that jazz. He explained, "We had a small emergency down at the station." "There's a problem with the newsroom's edit deck. Are you up to the challenge?"

"Bob," Gary moaned, pronouncing his name in two frustrated syllables: "Bah- ahb." Jeezus. I just finished two shifts in a row, and I have to pick up Gwen's friend from the airport in less an hour.

"How about Brian?" you might wonder. Gary was willing to help. "He should be able to fix a fucking jammed deck," says the narrator.

Bob scoffed, "Yeah, yeah." "With both hands and a map, Brian couldn't find his own ass."

"How are you doing?"

"I'd do it if I could," Bob replied. "However, Penny is sick, and who will look after the kids?" They won't be able to finish the editing without it. They'll be unable to deliver the news... " He applied it with a trowel, delivering the final line with genuine horror.

Gary smiled despite himself; without the eleven o'clock news, who knows where we'd be.

"All right," he admitted. "But that's all there is to it! I'm leaving after you fix the deck. There is no such thing as nonsense."

"You've figured it out!" Bob exhaled a sigh of relief. "Thanks, Gar; you're a good friend."

Gary grumbled, "Yes, yeah." "You owe me, motherfucker," says the narrator.

He turned off the phone and proceeded into the kitchen to deliver the news. Gwen was softly slamming things together, removing dishes from the drying rack and clicking mugs and plates with purpose.

"Uh, babe..." says the narrator.

She said, "I heard." "Mr. Devoted," says the narrator. She washed and racked the now-emptied coffee carafe with soapy water. She conveyed everything he needed to know in just two words. City of Eggshells.

He apologized, saying, "It's just a jammed deck." "I'll be back in plenty of time to get to the airport," says the narrator.

"It's OK," she said, implying that it isn't. "I'll go grab her on my own."

He immediately regretted saying, "I don't want you driving."

She took a glass and swished it swish. I don't give a damn what you want.

Gary took a step toward her, and Gwen smashed the glass almost to shattering. The meaning was crystal apparent, and the translation was the aloha of unspoken marriage-speak.

You perish if you touch me.

Gary took a step back. He couldn't think of anything else to say or do. This was a storm front that had to dissipate on its own hormonal terms.

"I'll be right back, darlin'," he promised. "Promise."

Gary snatched his leather jacket from the garage door entrance peg and quietly shut the door behind him. Gwen continued to wash and rinse, but her shoulders were slightly trembling. She wailed quietly, and the sound was drowned out by dishwashing clatter.

Gary's heart ached as he replaced the oil and prepared the bike. He felt sorry for the infant. When Spike finally appears, the world will be a much better place. For each of them, the final stretch was the most difficult.

He put on his riding gloves and leather jacket. His helmet rested on the seat's passenger hump. Gwen had given him a ninja-black road-warrior-style fiberglass monstrosity as a preventative pie-Day Father's gift. It was the kind of helmet that only rice-burner riders thought was cool, encasing his entire head and face with just a small snap-on plate for his eyes. He despised it, but was grateful to her for giving it to him.

Gary sat on the softtail, turned it on, and cranked it up; the engine screamed to life. It vibrated between Gary's thighs, making him feel instantly better and clearing his mind.

He shrugged and said, "Fuck it." All that nonsense goes into each existence. The sun would be shining when he returned if the gods of expectant fatherhood were on his side.

Gary revved the engine, backed out of the garage, and took to the road.

I'm right in the middle of it.